Fondue

Lenny Rice

Brigid Callinan

TEN SPEED PRESS
Berkeley

Ten Speed Press and the Ten Speed Press colophon are registered trademarks
of Random House, Inc.

Library of Congress Cataloging-in-Publication Data
Rice, Lenny.
  Fondue / Lenny Rice, Brigid Callinan.
      p. cm.
  Includes index.
  1. Fondue. I. Callinan, Brigid. II. Title.
  TX825.R53 2007
  641.8'1—dc22   2007010652

Hardcover ISBN: 978-1-58008-889-3

Printed in China

Cover and text design by Chloe Rawlins
Prop styling by Natalie Hoelen
Food styling by Kim Konecny
Food styling assistance by Julia Scahill
Photography assistance by Akiko Seki and Harumi
Food styling on page 96 and on the hardcover edition cover by Karen Shinto

11 10 9 8 7 6 5 4 3 2

First Edition

Fondue

Contents

Introduction

Okay, admit it: you've had a fondue pot in your garage/attic/basement since who knows when, likely a long-ago wedding/Christmas/housewarming gift, and you haven't had the heart to take it to Goodwill. It's still sitting there next to a Salad Shooter and electric knife. You've hung on to it all this time because you know in your heart that fondue is a great idea. But like every great idea, it needs to be dusted off, re-examined, and updated regularly to be appreciated.

A few years ago, after teaching a series of cheese classes, we found ourselves with a mountain of very delicious cheese scraps. To honor the memory of those cheeses, we impulsively decided to throw a fondue party. The outcome? We hit fondue-pot pay dirt in our circle of foodie friends. Why did everyone have a fondue pot that had never been used? Our hard-hitting investigative reporting uncovered a shocking fact: people had no fondue clue. Simply put, they did not know how to make fondue and consequently did not realize how easy and fun fondue can be! They associated fondue with leisure suits and shag carpet. Lenny and Brigid to the rescue! What followed was a hedonistic feast of melty, cheesy, chocolaty, and caramely delights, without a single leisure suit or a pair of Earth shoes in sight.

Needless to say, our inaugural fondue inspired many subsequent events just like it. Though we honor the classic fondue traditions at our fondue parties, we also experiment with our favorite foods of the moment and imagine many more tantalizing fondue combinations for future gatherings. This book is the culmination of those imaginings, meant to inspire a fresh, new look at an old favorite.

We don't want to risk overstating its power, but fondue is magic. Born out of winter resourcefulness in Alpine farmhouses, the communal fondue has always been at least as comforting socially as it is gastronomically. We would love to invite a bunch of sociologists to observe a fondue party. Maybe they could explain how fondue can transform a group of disparate social factions into a competitive yet cooperative cheesy love fest, bound by melted cheese and color-coded forks. At our fondue parties, we don't have to worry that all we have for dinner is bread, cheese, and a little wine; so we are able to truly celebrate the fun and warmth of both our friends and our fondue.

We want to share this fun with you. What's better than food on a stick? Fondue can be many things: an entire party (our preference), or an appetizer, entrée, or dessert. We have scoured the cheese-covered earth to bring you loads of options for sharing the magic of fondue with your friends and family.

Before You Dip

FONDUE PRIMER AND
PARTY PLANNING TIPS

The term fondue comes from the French word *fondre* (to melt). Dating back to eighteenth-century Switzerland, when the local cheese and wine were both common household ingredients, fondue started as a way for people in Alpine villages to utilize cheeses that had become hard and dry during winter storage. Each component of the fondue would have been readily available when little else was, and, while delicious, the additions were strictly functional: the wine in which the cheese is melted protected it from scorching over direct heat; kirsch, a cherry brandy, was added if the cheese lacked the desired tang; the cornstarch or flour kept the fat and protein in the cheese from separating.

Not much has changed in terms of what makes a great fondue today—a good cheese is still the most important ingredient. The good news is that we have more cheeses available to us than ever, and more places throughout the country to buy cheese for fondue. Explore your neighborhood to find the best cheese sources—grocery stores, specialty stores, wine stores. If you can't find what you desire locally, go online. You'll be amazed at the number of online vendors that will ship cheese right to your door.

BUYING AND STORING CHEESE

When deciding where to buy your cheese, most important to find out is how well the cheese has been cared for once it has left the farm or dairy. Here are some tips on how to get the best cheese for your fondue.

The best quality cheese will be cut to order from the original size wheel. This is not always an option, but if you can find a shop that sells cheese that way you will generally get a better piece of cheese. If the cheese is stored as a wheel, it retains its moisture and is less likely to absorb undesirable flavors from other foods in the refrigerator or from plastic wrap. If you can't find a shop that cuts to order, make sure you buy from one that sells a lot of cheese; this usually means the cut pieces haven't spent too much time wrapped in plastic and stored with other things that can impart unwanted flavors. As soon as cheese is cut, grated, or shaved, it begins to dry out; with the lost moisture goes the flavor, so also avoid purchasing any cheeses that have already been grated or shaved. Finally, purchase cheese as close as possible to when you plan to use it (most cheeses should be eaten within one to two weeks from the date of purchase), and get only the amount you need.

How much fondue to make for a party? Most of our recipes call for a pound of cheese and serve four to six people as an appetizer or party-snack portion, or two to three people as an entrée. For a party of ten to twelve people, we recommend serving at least three cheese fondue recipes with various accompaniments, along with one or two dessert fondues.

Cheese is a living thing and it needs to breathe. If the cheese was purchased wrapped in plastic, rewrap it in butcher or parchment paper when you get it home. If the parchment is very thin, however, give the cheese a double wrap or it will tend to dry out. Blue cheeses fare best when wrapped in aluminum foil. The best spot to store cheese is in the refrigerator, which is unfortunately colder than ideal, but the only option for most of us. More specifically, store it in the crisper drawer where it's a bit warmer and more humid (cheese absorbs moisture too) than in other spots in the fridge. If you're feeling extra protective, do all of the above (rewrap and keep in crisper) *and* store the cheese in a small, cardboard box, which will also protect it from other refrigerator odors. Never freeze cheese for any reason; you will be left with a dry crumbly mess when it thaws.

FONDUE COMPONENTS

Once you have chosen your cheese, making fondue is easy! Unless you use additional flavorings, fondue really has only three major components: cheese, liquid, and starch. Though the proportions of each ingredient may vary slightly depending on the variety of cheese you use, here is a good base formula for creating your own fondue recipe: one pound of cheese, one cup of liquid, and two tablespoons of flour. You can use almost any kind of cheese for fondue, but some melt better than others. The smoothest melters are semi-firm to firm, aged at least several months to a year, and moderately high in fat (around 40 percent). Cheeses that don't do as well in the fondue pot are crumbly cheeses like feta or varieties that are meant to maintain their texture somewhat when heated, like mozzarella and many of the Mexican cheeses. Very soft cheeses like fresh chèvre and triple-crèmes will require less liquid than aged varieties that are lower in moisture. Adjust your liquid by starting with a quarter cup and adding more if necessary.

Wine is the traditional liquid used in fondue, but ciders, beers, and low-acid juices like apple are all good fondue bases. Experiment with your favorite beverages. If you are using wine, choose one that doesn't have a particularly strong single flavor note, like grapefruit or oak. The predominant flavor will not diminish much and sometimes becomes stronger with cooking. In general, light, crisp white wines are best for fondue: sauvignon blanc, pinot grigio, and dry Riesling are all good choices. You may also want to add a small amount of acid to your fondue in the form of lemon or lime juice squeezed in at the end to brighten the flavor. The extra acid also helps prevent the fondue from separating, so you can add a little lemon juice to any fondue if it starts to separate and then stir it vigorously until it comes together.

We have used flour as the starch component for most of our recipes, but cornstarch, potato flour, and arrowroot will also work. Flour has a little less thickening power than the other starches and doesn't have to be mixed with cold liquid before adding to the fondue. Cornstarch, arrowroot, and potato flour should be made into a slurry with a small amount of your fondue's base liquid before adding to the hot fondue.

WHAT TO DIP?

We give specific recommendations for dippers with each recipe, but feel free to stray from our list if you get inspired. Experiment with your favorite flavors and you'll have more fun. When in doubt or short on time, you can always keep it simple with just bread and crackers. Use a sturdy bread with a good crust; toast it to keep it from breaking up in the fondue, either before or after cutting it into bite-size pieces. Breadsticks also make great dippers. For dessert fondues, choose cake that is dense, not crumbly; you can also toast cut cake pieces for easier dipping. Our sour cream (page 112) and devil's food pound cakes (page 111) are also great choices for most dessert fondues. To make party prep easier, they can be made ahead and frozen; just thaw them at room temperature for 6 to 8 hours. For variety, try the unexpected, like soft or crisp cookies, Rice Krispy treats, or donuts for your dessert fondues. Try our cinnamon-sugar donut holes (page 109) for an extra-special dipper.

Offer vegetables that are raw or cooked, but their texture should complement the fondue. We like to use crunchy raw vegetables with some of the stronger-flavored fondues, like Big Bacony Blue (page 73) and Midnight Moon at the Oasis (page 55); their crisp texture and bright flavor nicely balance the salty richness of the cheese. But we recommend cooking robust vegetables like cauliflower and broccoli to bring out their sweetness and improve their texture.

Fruit, both dried and fresh, is delicious with nearly any fondue. The only combinations we would warn against are citrus fruits or bananas with cheese fondue; otherwise, there is a world of possibilities. Here's a tip to prevent apples, pears, and bananas from browning after they're cut: dissolve a vitamin C tablet in one cup of water, put the solution in a clean spray bottle, and spray the fruit's cut surfaces. You can also use a teaspoon of lemon juice to a cup of water, but that can impart a lemony flavor you might not want.

Cured or roasted meats, sausages, and shrimp are nice additions to the fondue spread. Any meat or fish you use in cheese fondue should be cooked and cut into bite-size pieces, with the exception of shrimp, which can be left whole and peeled for easy dipping.

Toasted nuts, seeds, and coconut provide the crowning touch and a nice texture complement for savory or sweet fondues. Provide small dishes of these items so guests can top their gooey delights with either a dunk or a sprinkle. Toast coconut or nuts on a parchment-lined baking sheet in a 350-degree oven for 10 to 15 minutes, or until they smell toasty. Allow nuts and coconut to cool before placing them in serving dishes.

FONDUE POTS AND FUEL

Once you have the ingredients, all you need is a pot in which to conjure your fondue magic. If you really don't have a fondue pot in your garage, attic, or elsewhere, there are many sources, both actual and virtual, to meet your fondue equipment needs. Lenny's favorite fondue foraging site is eBay, where she has acquired an impressive collection of vintage fondue pots. Brigid favors Marshalls, TJ Maxx, Tuesday Morning, and Ross stores, with the philosophy that the hunt is at least half the fun (and you might find a great pair of shoes in the process). For those who want a more direct route to the perfect pot, retailers like Williams-Sonoma and Sur La Table carry a variety of beautiful sets in their stores and online.

Regardless of its source or style, the ideal pot for us is made of metal, like enameled cast iron, as it is heatproof and can safely go on the stove. That means you can cook and serve the fondue in the same pot. If a ceramic fondue pot is all you have, prepare the fondue as directed in a heavy saucepan and transfer it to the ceramic pot for serving. We do recommend a ceramic pot for the chocolate fondues in this book, as they can maintain a lower heat with the use of a candle rather than canned fuel.

Canned fondue fuel, or chafing fuel, is available in several forms at kitchenware stores, some supermarkets, and hardware stores, and of course, online. Most are an ethanol-based gel. Use the form and size recommended by the manufacturer of your fondue pot. The fuels can be dangerous; use great care when storing and lighting them. Don't store them near a heat source or in the drawer with your Strike Anywhere matches! Most modern pots use a two- to three-ounce can of paste-gel fuel, which can be purchased as refills in a pack of three. You will typically get 90 minutes to 2 hours of fondue heat out of a three-ounce can of fuel. If you have an older fondue pot, you may need bottled gel fuel or a larger can of paste-gel fuel, which also comes in an eight-ounce size. Use common sense and keep flammable materials away from the burning fuel. Extinguish the flame by smothering it with the can's lid.

PARTY PLANNING TIPS

You've got the cheese; you've got the fuel; now you can party! We know your fondue party will be *the* hot invitation of the season. Here are a few tips to start you on the path to being a fondue guru.

Do your homework: Most fondue prep can be done the night before a party, from cooking the vegetables to grating the cheese. About the only thing you can't do ahead is cut fruits that will oxidize, like apples and pears. Organize your prep so that lighting the Sterno is the only task left for you to do when your guests arrive.

Keep it covered: Fondue parties tend to inspire the sort of exuberance that can leave your furniture in need of a steam cleaning, so take preventive measures. Protect wood tables with colorful oilcloths, rather than your good linens. Provide guests with plenty of full-size napkins and use paper plates to avoid carpet dribbles. If you expect a really messy crowd, you may want to cover the floor underneath common dipping areas with inexpensive plastic shower-curtain liners.

Stick it to 'em: Provide each guest with his or her own fondue fork; if your forks aren't color-coded, get some craft tape, stickers, or ribbon in several colors to personalize them. A container with disposable bamboo skewers makes a handy backup.

Spread the love: Create different fondue stations around the party area, rather than grouping them in a central location. This encourages socializing and good people flow. Surround each fondue pot with its particular accompaniments, and provide extra serving containers of standards like bread and crackers all around the area. So that your guests can pace themselves, it's also a good idea to serve a few nonfondue foods, such as green or mixed vegetable salads, a piece of roasted meat, or some poached fish.

Set out drinks all around: Provide several beverage stations. Have easy access to your beverage assortment of choice—dish tubs filled with ice work well. Locate them strategically around the party area. Serve drinks in disposable cups (we like the clear hard plastic cocktail type) that guests can personalize with inexpensive stickers from the craft store that you provide. If you want to use stemware, give your guests identifying markers for their own glasses.

Have a theme: Everyone loves a theme party, especially if it involves cheese. Combine fondue recipes with a common thread, and decorate accordingly:

Latin Flavors = Queso Mi Mucho + Portuguesa do Sonoma + Cheese of La Mancha + Mexican Chocolate + Dulce de Leche

Après-Ski = Ski Haus Special + Nordic Nights + My Truffle Valentine + Chocolate Hazelnut with Frangelico + Caramel Latte

Americana = Big Bacony Blue + Combination Pizza Fondue + Philly's Phave + From the Malt Shop + Ode to a Candy Bar

Play nice: It's never fun to have too many rules, but there is some fondue etiquette that you should make obvious to your guests. No double dipping—one bite per dip. Provide guests with plates and utensils so they can dip their food and transfer it to the plate to eat with a fork if they prefer. The fork is for dipping, not for "lipping." Remind your guests not to touch the fork with their lips or tongue when enjoying their fondue.

Have a good soak: Anyone who has tried to scrape burnt cheese off a lasagna pan knows that it takes elbow grease. When your fondue pots are ready for the scullery, it is easiest to soak them overnight to loosen the hardened cheese. The next morning, use a small plastic bowl scraper to scrape off the softened cheese. If you are the type who just has to clean up the night of the party, white vinegar is the answer. The acid breaks down the protein in the cheese and it will come off pretty easily with a scrubby pad. Our old favorite S.O.S pad is another helpful tool in the cheese mitigation effort.

Forever Fondue

SAVORY CLASSICS

Nordic Nights

Maybe it's because the Scandinavian landscape seems like the perfect backdrop for a fondue party, chic or rustic. Maybe it was the influence of chef Marcus Samuelsson and food writer Andreas Viestad, two dreamy Scandinavians with whom we had the good fortune to work. Either way, a fondue celebration of the land of fjords and Vikings is in order. Scandinavians say that their traditional liquor, aquavit (from the Latin *aqua vitae*, water of life), will magically make room in your stomach for more delicious food; so in case your guests crave another dip of this fondue, be sure to have the bottle of aquavit at the ready.

1 pound Jarlsberg, grated

2 tablespoons all-purpose flour

1 cup unoaked or lightly oaked chardonnay

5 juniper berries

$1/2$ teaspoon caraway seed

$1/2$ teaspoon kosher salt

2 tablespoons aquavit

Toss the cheese with the flour in a bowl and set aside. In a fondue pot, combine the wine, juniper berries, caraway seed, and salt and bring to a simmer over medium-high heat. Decrease the heat to medium-low and let the pot sit for 10 minutes, then remove and discard the juniper berries. Add the cheese mixture to the pot, $1/2$ cup at a time, stirring to melt after each addition. Add the aquavit and stir until smooth. Serve immediately.

Makes 3 cups

SERVE WITH: toasted black, dark rye, or pumpernickel bread cubes • red or Yukon gold potatoes, steamed or roasted • steamed cauliflower florets • roasted beets • apple chunks • pear chunks

BEVERAGE SUGGESTIONS: white Burgundy • pilsner or lager beer • pinot blanc

CHEESE NOTES: A mild Swiss-style cheese originally made in the Norwegian county of the same name, Jarlsberg has a sweet, nutty flavor and large irregular holes. Jarlsberg is widely available in the United States, but if you can't find it, try Swiss, Comté, or Gruyère.

Ski Haus Special

We never get tired of the classics. This basic, very traditional fondue is always a hit. When you're down to the dregs at the end of the fondue party, here's a suggestion from our friend and Swiss-Austrian fondue guru Mark Dommen, chef at San Francisco's One Market Restaurant: when the fondue is almost gone but you still have some fuel left, add a whole egg or two to the super sticky cheese and stir gently until the egg is set but still soft.

1 pound cave-aged Gruyère, grated

2 tablespoons all-purpose flour

1 clove garlic, halved lengthwise

1 cup sauvignon blanc or other
   dry white wine

2 tablespoons kirsch

1 egg (optional)

Toss the cheese with the flour in a bowl and set aside. Rub the inside of a fondue pot with the cut sides of the garlic, then place the pieces in the pot. Add the wine and bring to a boil over medium-high heat. Decrease the heat to medium-low and add the cheese mixture, $1/2$ cup at a time, stirring until melted after each addition. Add the kirsch and stir to combine, then add the egg and stir until just cooked through. Serve immediately.

Makes 2$1/2$ cups

SERVE WITH: toasted rustic bread cubes • apple chunks • pear chunks • roasted or steamed red potatoes • assorted pickles

BEVERAGE SUGGESTIONS: dry riesling • sauvignon blanc • pinot noir

CHEESE NOTES: Gruyère is a versatile classic and one of the two cheeses used in traditional Swiss fondue (the other is Emmental). Its nutty, slightly fruity flavor and dense, smooth texture make it ideal for fruit and cheese trays, grilled cheese sandwiches, quiche, and, of course, fondue. As Gruyère ages, it becomes more pungent and complex, so buy one aged to your taste and recipe needs.

French Onion Fondue

We love the slab of gooey melted cheese on top of French onion soup—come on, who cares about the soup? Cheese front and center, this fondue captures the essence of the original in a new (and for us, improved) form—without all that unnecessary liquid. Caramelizing the onion slices takes a little extra time, but it is well worth the effort. So be patient until they are nice and brown, which makes them meltingly tender and extra sweet. Here we call for one of our favorite cheeses, Comté, the French version of Swiss cheese; but Gruyère, the "true" Swiss cheese, is also delicious. This fondue will be thick and stringy—you will want to have a cheese-stretching competition when you serve it!

1 pound Comté or Gruyère, grated

1 tablespoon all-purpose flour

2 tablespoons unsalted butter

1 onion, cut in half and thinly sliced crosswise

1 tablespoon fresh thyme leaves, minced

1¼ cups dry sherry

Toss the cheese with the flour in a bowl and set aside. In a fondue pot, melt the butter over medium heat. Add the onion and cook, stirring frequently, until golden brown and very soft, 20 to 30 minutes. Add the thyme and stir until incorporated. Add the sherry and increase the heat to medium-high, stirring constantly. When the liquid just begins to boil, decrease the heat to medium-low and add the cheese mixture, ½ cup at a time, stirring until melted after each addition. Serve immediately.

Makes 3 cups

SERVE WITH: toasted rustic bread cubes

BEVERAGE SUGGESTIONS: chardonnay • pinot noir • light-bodied merlot

CHEESE NOTES: Comté is the French version of Gruyère. It is named for Franche-Comté, the region of France where it is made solely from the milk of the Montbéliard cow and then aged a minimum of six months to develop its characteristic hazelnut flavor. Regional dairies still make Comté in small quantities in traditional copper kettles.

Ye Olde English Pub Special

There is no better place on earth to drink beer than a dark, cozy British pub. Some tasty pub grub washed down with a sturdy ale is the ideal antidote to the damp English winter. This fondue is a salute to the crowning achievements of English cuisine: beer and cheese.

1 pound red Cheshire or sharp
   Cheddar, grated
2 tablespoons all-purpose flour
1 cup English or Scottish ale
1 teaspoon kosher salt

Toss the cheese with the flour in a bowl and set aside. In a fondue pot, add the ale and salt and bring to a boil over medium-high heat. Decrease the heat to medium-low and add the cheese mixture, $1/2$ cup at a time, stirring until melted after each addition. Serve immediately.

Makes 2^1/$_2$ cups

SERVE WITH: Irish soda bread cubes (page 108) • toasted whole grain and rustic bread cubes • assorted crackers • apple chunks • pear chunks • cooked British bangers (sausages), cut into bite-size chunks • boiled red or Yukon gold potatoes

BEVERAGE SUGGESTIONS: ale or stout • sauvignon blanc • tawny port

CHEESE NOTES: Cheshire is a Cheddar-style English cheese whose sharp, savory flavor comes from the abundant salt deposits in the areas where the cattle graze. The addition of annatto, a natural coloring for cheese derived from the seeds of the achiote tree, gives red Cheshire its rich hue. This cheese makes a beautiful, deep reddish-orange fondue.

Autumn in Vermont

Vermont's charms are many and hard to resist. We both fell in love with the Green Mountain State while at cooking school and have fond memories of Lake Champlain, leaf season, and Ben and Jerry's tours. We adore the Vermont autumn and created this fondue to remind us of Vermont's beauty, warmth, and flavor.

1 pound Shelburne Farms Vermont Cheddar or other sharp white Cheddar, grated

2 tablespoons all-purpose flour

1 cup hard apple cider

1 teaspoon apple-cider vinegar

Toss the cheese with the flour in a bowl and set aside. In a fondue pot, bring the cider to a boil over medium-high heat. Decrease the heat to low and add the cheese mixture, $1/2$ cup at a time, stirring until melted after each addition. Add the vinegar and stir until smooth. Serve immediately.

Makes 3 cups

SERVE WITH: toasted rustic bread cubes • apple chunks • steamed broccoli florets • ham, cut into bite-size cubes • chopped toasted walnuts

BEVERAGE SUGGESTIONS: dry hard cider (try Vermont's own Woodchuck brand) • syrah/shiraz • ruby port

CHEESE NOTES: Shelburne Farms is a working farm and environmental education center on the shore of Lake Champlain. It also happens to make killer Cheddar cheese with milk from its herd of grass-grazed Swiss Brown cows. If you're ever in Vermont, you can visit the farm and watch them make it.

California Cheddar-Apple

Tart apples + salty Cheddar = heaven. Here we show off Bravo Cheddar with the classic complement of apples in the form of juice as its base.

1 pound Bravo Farms Cheddar or other sharp Cheddar, grated

1 tablespoon all-purpose flour

³/₄ cup apple juice

Toss the cheese with the flour in a bowl and set aside. In a fondue pot, bring the apple juice to a boil over medium-high heat. Decrease the heat to low and add the cheese mixture, ¹/₂ cup at a time, stirring until melted after each addition. Serve immediately.

Makes 2 cups

SERVE WITH: toasted bread cubes • steamed broccoli florets • steamed cauliflower florets • ham, cut into bite-size cubes • cooked chicken-apple sausages, cut into bite-size pieces • apple chunks • pear chunks

BEVERAGE SUGGESTIONS: sauvignon blanc • gamay (Beaujolais) • hard or nonalcoholic cider

CHEESE NOTES: In California's San Joaquin Valley, vast factory dairies are the standard, which is why we love Visalia's Bravo Farms farmstead cheeses. Surrounded by enormous tracts of industrial dairy, Bravo raises hormone-free Jersey cows and produces superb traditional farmhouse Cheddar from the rich, high-protein Jersey milk.

The Luck of the Dutch

Lucky you if you've had the chance to visit Ireland's beautiful County Cork, where dairy cows graze on rolling green hills in the shadow of Blarney Castle. From Northwest Cork comes Coolea, an Irish version of Holland's Gouda. We pair Coolea here with another Dutch classic, Heineken beer. Bringing nations together, that's what fondue is all about!

1 pound Coolea, Gouda, or Edam cheese, grated

2 tablespoons all-purpose flour

1 cup beer (Heineken or other pale lager)

Toss the cheese with the flour in a bowl and set aside. In a fondue pot, bring the beer to a boil over medium-high heat. Decrease the heat to medium-low and add the cheese mixture, $1/2$ cup at a time, stirring until melted after each addition. Serve immediately.

Makes 2 cups

SERVE WITH: Irish brown soda bread cubes (page 108) • toasted wheat or walnut bread cubes • apple chunks • boiled red or Yukon gold potatoes • roasted or boiled onions • cooked Irish sausages or bacon, cut into bite-size pieces

BEVERAGE SUGGESTIONS: brown ale • Amontillado sherry • blanc de noirs (sparkling wine)

CHEESE NOTES: The Willems family swapped a hectic life in the Amsterdam restaurant business for a farm in the remote countryside of Northwestern County Cork, Ireland. Today they produce Coolea, a Dutch Gouda-style cheese named after the tiny Irish village they now call home. Though it is very much like traditional Dutch Gouda, Coolea has a creamier texture and a nuttier, more caramel-like flavor. It makes a fantastic fondue.

Irish Cheddar and Stout

We included this Irish fondue recipe at the risk of being reprimanded by Brigid's extensive Irish family for the misuse of a perfectly good half pint of stout. But in combination with the browned onions and lively Irish Cheddar, the stout does flavorful service to the fondue tradition. And you'll have a half pint extra to fortify you in the grueling task of stirring in the cheese.

1 pound Irish Cheddar (such as Dubliner), grated

2 tablespoons all-purpose flour

1 tablespoon unsalted butter

1 onion, diced

$1/2$ teaspoon kosher salt

1 tablespoon coarse-grain mustard

$1^1/4$ cups Irish stout (such as Guinness or Murphy's)

Toss the cheese with the flour in a bowl and set aside. In a fondue pot, melt the butter over medium heat. Add the onion and cook, stirring frequently, until golden brown and very soft, about 10 minutes. Add the salt, mustard, and stout. Increase the heat to medium-high, stirring constantly, until the liquid boils. Decrease the heat to medium-low and add the cheese mixture, $1/2$ cup at a time, stirring until melted after each addition. Serve immediately.

Makes 3 cups

SERVE WITH: Irish brown soda bread cubes (page 108) • cooked garlic or chicken-apple sausages, cut into bite-size pieces • steamed red or Yukon gold potatoes • boiled spring or pearl onions • steamed brussels sprouts

BEVERAGE SUGGESTIONS: stout or ale • hard cider • sauvignon blanc

CHEESE NOTES: When you think of great Cheddar producers, you need only consider the world's premier beer drinking regions. The Irish, worthy contenders in the beer drinking department, produce delicious traditional Cheddar cheeses that are perfectly suited to enjoying with a fluffy pint of Guinness. Look for Kerrygold and Dubliner, two widely available brands.

Haarlem Shuffle

In this fondue we used a sharp (aged six months) Gouda and the traditional Dutch accompaniment of cumin seed for a unique and hearty flavor. If you really want to "go Dutch," try finishing the fondue with a splash of good gin.

1 pound Winchester Farms Gouda or other Gouda, grated

2 tablespoons all-purpose flour

1 tablespoon cumin seed

1 cup dry Alsatian riesling

2 tablespoons freshly squeezed lemon juice

Toss the cheese with the flour in a bowl and set aside. Heat a fondue pot over medium-high heat; add the cumin seed, stirring frequently until it darkens slightly and smells toasty, about 3 to 4 minutes. Add the wine and bring to a boil. Decrease the heat to low and add the cheese mixture, $1/2$ cup at a time, stirring until melted after each addition. Add the lemon juice and stir until smooth. Serve immediately.

Makes 3 cups

SERVE WITH: toasted rustic bread cubes • steamed cauliflower florets • cooked garlic sausages, cut into bite-size pieces • roasted red or Yukon gold potatoes

BEVERAGE SUGGESTIONS: pinot noir • dry riesling • Belgian-style ale

CHEESE NOTES: We're glad Jules Wesselink, owner of Winchester Farms in California's Riverside County, opted to make cheese rather than retire and say good-bye to his dairy cows. At an age when he should have been thinking about golf and a life of leisure, he decided to return to his native Haarlem, Holland, and learn how to make Gouda. And what Gouda it is! Winchester Gouda is available at various levels of aging, and all are delicious.

Jack of All Chiles

We often make this fondue for a productive afternoon of watching sports on TV. It's like a do-it-yourself enchilada: cheesy and spicy, but without the unnecessary complication of all that rolling and baking. Serve it with pickled jalapeños for a triple-chile experience.

1¼ cups beer (preferably ale)

2 cloves garlic, minced

1 (4-ounce) can mild diced green chiles

1½ pounds Vella Cheese Company Jalapeño Jack or other pepper jack cheese, grated

1 teaspoon ground cumin

2 teaspoons freshly squeezed lime juice

In a fondue pot, combine the beer, garlic, and chiles and bring to a simmer over medium-high heat. Decrease the heat to medium-low and add the cheese, ½ cup at a time, stirring until melted after each addition. Add the cumin and lime juice and stir until smooth. Serve immediately.

Makes 3 cups

SERVE WITH: tortilla chips • cooked chorizo sausages, cut into bite-size pieces • celery sticks • pickled jalapeños • cherry tomatoes • minced toasted pumpkin seeds

BEVERAGE SUGGESTIONS: ale or lager • pinot blanc • riesling

CHEESE NOTES: A cheese native to California, jack is said to have been created in Monterey County in the 1890s. Vella Jalapeño Jack cheese is made in Sonoma, California, by Vella Cheese Company. This younger, softer version of jack is made of cow's milk and aged only a few weeks. While cutting the curd, Vella adds chopped jalapeños to give it an extra kick.

Cheese of La Mancha

Spain's tapas restaurants were Lenny's favorite destination on her first trip to Europe. This savory combination is a pot full of her Spanish *bocadillo* flavor memories, with the delicious anchovy featured prominently. Though chèvre, a fresh goat cheese, is not a traditional Spanish ingredient, it mellows the fondue's saltiness and contributes to its creamy texture.

1 clove garlic, halved lengthwise

1 cup Italian or Spanish dry white wine

12 ounces Manchego, grated

8 ounces chèvre, crumbled

4 to 6 anchovies, minced

2 teaspoons sherry vinegar

Kosher salt (optional)

Rub the inside of a fondue pot with the cut sides of the garlic, then place the pieces in the pot. Add the wine and bring it to a simmer over medium-high heat. Decrease the heat to medium-low and add the Manchego, $1/2$ cup at a time, stirring until melted after each addition. Add the chèvre and stir until smooth, then stir in the anchovies and vinegar. Season with salt to taste. Serve immediately.

Makes 3 cups

SERVE WITH: toasted rustic bread cubes •
cooked chorizo sausages cut into bite-size
pieces • roasted red or Yukon gold potatoes • cherry tomatoes • radishes

BEVERAGE SUGGESTIONS: tempranillo •
Amontillado sherry • fruity merlot

CHEESE NOTES: Spain's most famous
cheese, Manchego, is one of the
most available Spanish cheeses in the
United States. Made from the milk of
Manchega sheep that graze the rocky
La Mancha countryside, Manchego
is available in different states of
maturity, from three months to one
year. For this recipe we recommend
a six-month or younger Manchego,
as it will melt more smoothly than the
aged varieties.

Pot of Gold

FONDUE GOES GOURMET

Champagne Velvet

A fun little four-pack of Rubicon Estates Sofia Blanc de Blancs inspired Lenny to create this velvety fondue indulgence. The base is Taleggio, one of her favorite Italian cheeses. Taleggio is available at varying stages of ripeness, and we recommend a younger, firmer one for this recipe. It will be easiest to remove the rind and cut up the Taleggio while it is very cold.

20 ounces Taleggio, rind discarded
and cubed
2 tablespoons all-purpose flour
1 cup blanc de blancs (sparkling wine)

Toss the cheese with the flour in a bowl and set aside. In a fondue pot, bring the wine to a boil over medium-high heat. Decrease the heat to low and add the cheese mixture, $1/2$ cup at a time, stirring until melted after each addition. Serve immediately.

Makes 3 cups

SERVE WITH: toasted baguette cubes • grapes • apple chunks • pear chunks • fresh figs, quartered • spears of Belgian endive • roasted onion quarters • chopped toasted walnuts

BEVERAGE SUGGESTIONS: off-dry gewürztraminer or riesling • prosecco • blanc de blancs (sparkling wine)

CHEESE NOTES: From Italy's Lombardy region, Taleggio is a rich, semi-soft cheese with a thin rind of orange mold. Though it has a pungent aroma, its flavor is sweet and mild, with a hint of yeastiness. It gets runnier and more flavorful as it ages. Excellent with fruit, Taleggio is also traditionally served with bitter salad greens like radicchio.

Benedictine and Beer

Beer, polka, Laverne and Shirley—Wisconsin has it all! We continue America's Dairyland beer and cheese tradition with this delicious fondue made from Wisconsin's Carr Valley Benedictine cheese. With its intoxicating aroma and thick, rich texture, it may just inspire you to polka the night away!

1 pound Carr Valley Benedictine, grated

2 tablespoons all-purpose flour

$2/3$ cup beer

Toss the cheese with the flour in a bowl and set aside. In a fondue pot, bring the beer to a boil over medium-high heat. Decrease the heat to low and add the cheese mixture, $1/2$ cup at a time, stirring until melted after each addition. Serve immediately.

Makes 2$1/2$ cups

SERVE WITH: toasted rustic bread cubes (walnut or whole grain is delicious) • Asian pear chunks • apple chunks • pitted dates • pitted prunes • mild salami, cut into bite-size pieces • cooked bratwurst, cut into bite-size pieces

BEVERAGE SUGGESTIONS: red Bordeaux • red Rhône • zinfandel

CHEESE NOTES: Some cheeses just have to be the center of attention. Benedictine is one of those cheeses. The Carr Valley Cheese Company in La Valle, Wisconsin, today led by Master Cheesemaker Sid Cook, has followed traditional methods for more than one hundred years to make unique cheeses like this one. Benedictine, a washed-rind cheese made of goat's, sheep's, and cow's milk, is one of Carr Valley's most interesting, with a rich, intense, meaty flavor that pairs well with full-bodied red wines.

Norman Conquest

The French region of Normandy is known for its apples, pastries, and sinfully creamy and delicious cheeses. In honor of those hardworking Norman cows, this fondue features Normandy's most famous cheese, Camembert, and the wickedly garlicky Boursin, a fresh cheese from Normandy that can be found in a little white box in most American supermarkets. Try it on apples and wash it down with a shot of calvados, the fiery Norman apple brandy.

10 ounces Camembert, rind discarded and cubed

2 tablespoons all-purpose flour

1 cup Chablis or chardonnay

1 (5.2-ounce) box Boursin

2 tablespoons muscat or other sweet dessert wine

Kosher salt (optional)

Toss the Camembert with the flour in a bowl and set aside. In a fondue pot, bring the Chablis to a boil over medium-high heat. Decrease the heat to low; add the Boursin, stirring until melted. Add the Camembert mixture, $1/2$ cup at a time, and stir until melted after each addition. Add the muscat and stir until smooth. Season with salt to taste. Serve immediately.

Makes 3 cups

SERVE WITH: apple chunks • cooked sausages, cut into bite-size pieces • roasted red or Yukon gold potatoes • cauliflower florets • toasted bread cubes

BEVERAGE SUGGESTIONS: calvados • dry hard cider • Champagne • Belgian-style beer

CHEESE NOTES: A soft-ripened cheese with a thick, white, bloomy rind, Camembert was first made in Normandy in 1791. It becomes softer and runnier as it ages, which is why it is said to have inspired the "melting" watches in Salvador Dalí's famous painting *The Persistence of Memory*.

California Country Roads

Producers of some of our favorite artisan cheeses, Cowgirl Creamery and Bellwether Farms are country neighbors just a half hour's drive apart on winding Northern California back roads. In this fondue, the full-flavored, washed-rind Red Hawk from Cowgirl Creamery is nicely balanced by Bellwether Farms's buttery, smooth Carmody. A splash of sweet wine complements both cheeses.

1 (12-ounce) round Cowgirl Creamery Red Hawk, rind discarded and cubed

8 ounces Bellwether Farms Carmody, grated

2 tablespoons all-purpose flour

1 cup Napa or Sonoma sauvignon blanc

2 tablespoons muscat or other sweet dessert wine

Toss the cheeses with the flour in a bowl and set aside. In a fondue pot, bring the sauvignon blanc to a boil over medium-high heat. Decrease the heat to low and add the cheese mixture, 1/2 cup at a time, stirring until melted after each addition. Add the muscat and stir until smooth. Serve immediately.

Makes 2 cups

SERVE WITH: toasted walnut or other rustic bread cubes • pear chunks • apple chunks • fresh figs, quartered • fig bars • Graham crackers

BEVERAGE SUGGESTIONS: pinot noir • blanc de noirs (sparkling wine) • fino sherry

CHEESE NOTES: Red Hawk is a triple-crème cheese washed with a brine solution that promotes the growth of beautiful red-orange bacteria on the rind. It's made with organic milk from Marin County's Straus Family Creamery, located right up the road from the Cowgirl Creamery dairy in Point Reyes Station. If you are not able to find Red Hawk, substitute Italian Taleggio or Robiola, or the French Époisses. Made with rich milk from Jersey cows, Bellwether's Carmody is an Italian-style cheese with a golden rind and a buttery texture that is balanced by a slightly tangy flavor—perfect for a grilled cheese sandwich.

My Truffle Valentine

Italy's Piedmont region is home to some of the world's most delicious foods—miraculous white truffles, incredible wines, and cheeses made of milk from the best-fed cows around. This fondue is perfect for special occasions; its luxurious texture and intoxicating truffle flavor and aroma will be the highlight of your celebration.

1 pound Bra Tenero, Fontina d'Aosta, or Toma, grated

2 tablespoons all-purpose flour

1 cup trebbiano or other light, fruity white wine

1 teaspoon white truffle oil

Toss the cheese with the flour together in a bowl and set aside. In a fondue pot, bring the wine to a boil over medium-high heat. Decrease the heat to low and add the cheese mixture, $1/2$ cup at a time, stirring until melted after each addition. Add the truffle oil and stir until smooth. Serve immediately.

Makes $2^1/2$ cups

SERVE WITH: toasted rustic bread cubes • roasted red or Yukon gold potatoes • roasted or steamed asparagus • steamed cauliflower florets • canned artichoke hearts

BEVERAGE SUGGESTIONS: sangiovese (Chianti) • Piemontese barolo or barbaresco • Champagne

CHEESE NOTES: Bra is both an Italian city in the Piedmont region (the self-proclaimed Cheese Capital of Europe) and the strictly regulated DOC (Denominazione di Origine Controllata) designation of the local cheeses. Bra Tenero (tenero is Italian for "tender" or "mild") is a sweet, elegant, and rich cow's milk cheese that we think is perfect for just about everything. For silken fondue to the best panini you can imagine, Bra is destined to become your new favorite cheese. Bra Duro, a more piquant and robust, longer-aged form, makes an excellent grating cheese. If you can't find Bra for this recipe, Italian Fontina is a good substitute.

Wild and Funky Fungi

Here's a fondue to try out on your more adventuresome friends who love a good strong cheese. Some may call it "stinky," but we just call it a delicious dinner. Porcini, chanterelle, and morel mushrooms all work well in this recipe, but portobellos or cremini will suffice if you can't find anything more exotic.

1 pound raclette, grated

1 teaspoon all-purpose flour

2 tablespoons olive oil

2 cups finely chopped wild mushrooms

Kosher salt and freshly ground
　　black pepper

1 cup marsanne, roussanne, viognier, or
　　other Rhône-style white wine

Toss the cheese with the flour in a bowl and set aside. In a fondue pot, heat the oil over high heat until it just starts to smoke. Add the mushrooms and stir to coat with oil. Season with salt and pepper to taste. Cook the mushrooms, stirring occasionally, until most of their liquid has evaporated, 7 to 10 minutes. Add the wine and bring to a boil. Decrease the heat to medium-low and add the cheese mixture, $1/2$ cup at a time, stirring until melted after each addition. Serve immediately.

Makes $3^1/2$ cups

SERVE WITH: toasted baguette cubes • roasted or boiled red potatoes • assorted pickles • boiled pearl onions • cooked garlic sausages or bratwurst, cut into bite-size chunks

BEVERAGE SUGGESTIONS: dry rosé • pinot noir • chenin blanc

CHEESE NOTES: Made in the Alps of France and Switzerland, raclette is a very pungent, semi-firm cow's milk cheese that, when heated, unleashes an aromatic wave of heavenly (to us) "barnyard magic" that can be enjoyed from several rooms away.

Bavarian Blue with Roasted Garlic

The tangy blue flavor of Cambozola pairs well with the sweet roasted garlic and provides a delicious foil for dried fruits like figs, dates, and prunes. Serve it with toasted walnut or raisin bread for a special treat.

1¼ pounds Cambozola, rind discarded and cubed

2 tablespoons all-purpose flour

¼ cup gewürztraminer, preferably German

8 to 10 cloves roasted garlic, chopped (see page 80)

Kosher salt (optional)

Toss the cheese with the flour in a bowl and set aside. In a fondue pot, bring the wine to a boil over medium-high heat. Decrease the heat to medium-low and add the cheese mixture, ½ cup at a time, stirring until melted after each addition. Add the roasted garlic and stir until smooth. Season with salt to taste. Serve immediately.

Makes 3 cups

SERVE WITH: toasted bread cubes (wheat and walnut breads are great) • grapes • apple chunks • pear chunks • dried or fresh figs • dates • prunes • chopped toasted walnuts, hazelnuts, or pecans

BEVERAGE SUGGESTIONS: off-dry or late-harvest gewürztraminer • Sauternes • viognier

CHEESE NOTES: From Germany, Cambozola is a mild and creamy blue-veined cheese with soft white mold coating. Created in the 1970s as a hybrid of Camembert and Gorgonzola, Cambozola is one of Germany's most popular cheeses.

A Sweet Blue Pear

To us, one of the world's great food combinations is pears and blue cheese. The sweet-salty, creamy-juicy counterpoints satisfy all our cravings. Good alternatives to Gorgonzola *dolce* are the Irish Cashel Blue and the French Fourme d'Ambert.

$^1\!/_2$ cup pear brandy or liqueur

$1^1\!/_4$ pounds Gorgonzola *dolce*, rind discarded and cubed

Freshly ground black pepper

In a fondue pot, bring the brandy to a boil over medium-high heat. Decrease the heat to low and add the cheese, $^1\!/_2$ cup at a time, stirring until melted after each addition. Season with pepper to taste. Serve immediately.

Makes 2 cups

SERVE WITH: toasted walnut bread cubes • Graham crackers • English whole wheat crackers or biscuits • fig bars and/or apple bars • pear chunks • apple chunks • fresh or dried figs, quartered • chopped toasted pecans, hazelnuts, or walnuts

BEVERAGE SUGGESTIONS: vin santo • Sauternes • tawny port

CHEESE NOTES: Named for the town near Milan, Italy, where it is made, Gorgonzola is produced with the same strain of penicillin mold as Roquefort. Gorgonzola *dolce* is younger, softer, and creamier than Gorgonzola *piccante* or *naturale*, which is aged at least 90 days. Both are delicious, especially as dessert cheeses with fruits and walnut bread and sweet-tart dessert wine like vin santo.

Pyrenees Pimentón

Since we discovered pimentón de la Vera, the Spanish smoked paprika, few dishes have escaped our kitchens without it. We find that its warm, sweet-smoky flavor improves everything we use it in: soups, potatoes, croutons, marinades. You may find pimentón at your grocery store in the spice section, but if not, check Resources (see page 117) for good online pimentón sources. Once you discover pimentón's charms, you'll want to use it in everything, too.

1 pound P'tit Basque, Ossau-Iraty, or other semi-firm sheep's milk cheese, rind discarded, and grated

1 tablespoon all-purpose flour

2 cloves garlic, halved

1 cup albariño or sauvignon blanc

1 teaspoon pimentón de la Vera

$1/2$ teaspoon ground cumin

2 tablespoons oloroso or Amontillado (not dry) sherry

Toss the cheese with the flour in a bowl and set aside. Rub the inside of the fondue pot with the cut sides of the garlic, then place the pieces in the pot. In a small bowl, form a paste by combining 1 tablespoon of the wine with the pimentón and cumin and set aside. Add the remaining wine to the fondue pot and bring to a simmer over medium-high heat. Decrease the heat to medium-low and add the spice paste, stirring until smooth. Add the cheese mixture, $1/2$ cup at a time, stirring until melted after each addition. Add the sherry and stir to combine. Serve immediately.

Makes 3 cups

continued

SERVE WITH: toasted rustic bread cubes • large pimiento-stuffed Spanish green olives • cooked, peeled shrimp • cooked chorizo sausages, cut into bite-size pieces • red or Yukon gold potatoes, roasted or boiled • chopped toasted marcona almonds (see Resources, page 115)

BEVERAGE SUGGESTIONS: albariño • dry rosé • dry cava (Spanish sparkling wine)

CHEESE NOTES: P'tit Basque and Ossau-Iraty are sheep's milk cheeses from the French Basque region, and cousins to the Spanish classic Manchego. Softer and more subtly flavored than Manchego, their smooth, creamy texture and subtle nuttiness make them excellent choices for people who *think* they don't like sheep's milk cheese.

Spring Forward

Fresh green vegetables, tarragon, and sheep's milk cheese *are* spring to us. This fondue is a great Easter appetizer. Have fun at the farmers' market with all the beautiful spring offerings to inspire your dipping.

1 pound Ossau-Iraty, P'tit Basque, Abbaye de Bellocq, Panache d'Aramitz, or other semi-firm sheep's milk cheese, grated

2 tablespoons all-purpose flour

1 clove garlic, halved lengthwise

1¼ cups dry riesling

1 sprig fresh tarragon, plus 1 tablespoon minced tarragon leaves

2 tablespoons Pernod

Toss the cheese with the flour in a bowl and set aside. Rub the inside of the fondue pot with the cut sides of the garlic, then place the pieces in the pot. Add the wine and the tarragon sprig and bring to a simmer over medium-high heat. Decrease the heat to medium-low and remove the tarragon sprig. Add the cheese mixture to the pot, ½ cup at a time, stirring until melted after each addition. Add the minced tarragon and Pernod and stir to combine. Serve immediately.

Makes 2 cups

SERVE WITH: toasted baguette cubes • raw or steamed fennel strips • canned artichoke hearts • steamed asparagus • boiled red or Yukon gold potatoes

BEVERAGE SUGGESTIONS: sauvignon blanc • chenin blanc • grüner veltliner

CHEESE NOTES: Ossau-Iraty is an AOC raw sheep's milk cheese from France's Basque region. Shepherds in the high fields of the Pyrenees make it as a way of preserving the summer milk from their flocks.

Sonoma Gardens

In Bay Area yards, rosemary plants and lemon trees grow like weeds, so we always have seasonings at our fingertips. Lenny has both Meyer lemons and rosemary in her backyard. She created this fondue as a tribute to our beautiful adopted home using cheeses from two Sonoma producers that are also right in our backyard, Vella Cheese Company and Bellwether Farms. The Meyer lemon, a mandarin-lemon hybrid, is particularly prolific in Napa and Sonoma and has a unique floral aroma and flavor. If you can't find Meyer lemons, this fondue is also delicious with the ubiquitous Eureka variety.

10 ounces Vella Cheese Company Dry Jack Special Select, grated

6 ounces Bellwether Farms Crescenza, cut into pieces

2 tablespoons all-purpose flour

1 cup viognier or other Rhône-style white wine

1 tablespoon minced fresh rosemary

Grated zest of 1 Meyer or Eureka lemon

1 tablespoon freshly squeezed Meyer or Eureka lemon juice

Kosher salt

Toss the cheeses with the flour in a bowl and set aside. In a fondue pot, bring the wine to a boil over medium-high heat. Decrease the heat to medium-low and add the cheese mixture, $1/2$ cup at a time, stirring until melted after each addition. Add the rosemary, lemon zest, and lemon juice and stir until smooth. Season with salt to taste. Serve immediately.

Makes 2 cups

SERVE WITH: toasted rustic bread cubes • steamed cauliflower florets • roasted red or Yukon gold potatoes • red bell pepper chunks

BEVERAGE SUGGESTIONS: viognier • white Burgundy • blanc de blancs (sparkling wine)

CHEESE NOTES: A pioneer in the California artisan cheese movement, Vella Cheese Company specializes in jack cheese, which it ages to perfection in an old brewery in downtown Sonoma. Dry Jack Special Select, akin to Parmigiano-Reggiano in texture and flavor, is produced in large wheels that are rubbed with a mixture of vegetable oil, cocoa, and black pepper, then aged at least twelve months. If you can't find Vella Dry Jack, substitute Parmigiano-Reggiano or another hard grating cheese such as asiago. Crescenza is a super-creamy soft cheese made by Bellwether Farms in gorgeous western Sonoma County, a few miles from the ocean. Bellwether was the first sheep dairy in California and produces some of the finest sheep's milk cheese around. They make Crescenza from the high-fat milk of Jersey cows that graze at a neighboring farm.

Portuguesa do Sonoma

The piquant olives and rich but tangy Portuguese-style cheese in this recipe call for a crisp, acidic white wine. To keep things Portuguese, we used vinho verde, a light, fruity, slightly effervescent white from Northwest Portugal's wine-growing region Entre-Douro-e-Minho. Reasonably priced and light in alcohol, vinho verde is also great as an aperitif or with seafood.

1 pound St. George or aged Cheddar, grated

2 tablespoons all-purpose flour

1 cup vinho verde, sauvignon blanc, or pinot blanc

1 cup pitted green olives, minced

Toss the cheese with the flour in a bowl and set aside. In a fondue pot, bring the wine to a boil over medium-high heat. Decrease the heat to low and add the cheese mixture, $1/2$ cup at a time, stirring until melted after each addition. Stir in the olives until combined. Serve immediately.

Makes 3 cups

SERVE WITH: toasted rustic bread cubes • cooked linguiça sausages, cut into bite-size pieces • roasted red or Yukon gold potatoes • cherry tomatoes

BEVERAGE SUGGESTIONS: pinot noir • sangiovese • zinfandel

CHEESE NOTES: The Matos family made cheese in the Azores for five generations. Lucky for us that they decided to move to Sonoma County, where they produce St. George, based on a recipe for Sao Jorge, a traditional Portuguese cheese. The fifteen-pound wheels of St. George are golden and dotted with tiny holes, with a nicely balanced flavor and a rich, slightly crumbly texture.

Mediterranean Holiday

We originally created this fondue full of sunny Italian flavors as yet another use for surplus summer tomatoes. But it's also great in the dead of winter, when you're craving a Mediterranean getaway (thank goodness for hothouse basil!). Pantaleo is one of the few goat's milk cheeses available from Italy and is worth seeking out (see Resources, page 115). If you can't find it, though, a young pecorino will work.

3 cloves garlic, chopped

1 cup pinot grigio

1 pound Pantaleo or young pecorino, grated

2 tablespoons minced fresh basil

In a fondue pot, add the garlic and wine and bring to a boil over medium-high heat. Decrease the heat to medium-low and add the cheese, 1/2 cup at a time, stirring until melted. Add the basil and stir to combine. Serve immediately.

Makes 3 cups

SERVE WITH: toasted rustic bread cubes • cherry tomatoes or beefsteak tomatoes, cut into bite-size pieces • roasted red or Yukon gold potatoes • grilled zucchini, cut into bite-size pieces

BEVERAGE SUGGESTIONS: zinfandel or primitivo • Chianti • dry Italian rosé

CHEESE NOTES: A raw goat's milk cheese from Sardinia, Pantaleo develops its sweet, complex flavor over 100 days of aging. Pantaleo is delicious with tomatoes and Mediterranean herbs such as oregano and basil. It also makes an excellent final course with wildflower honey and toasted nuts.

Goat of the Greek Isles

We have always loved pairing tangy goat cheese with bright Mediterranean flavors like oregano, olives, and tomatoes. Beautiful as well as tasty, this fondue also makes a super-quick pasta sauce tossed with hot fettucine or penne. Add more olives or tomatoes to taste, if you like.

8 ounces Comté, Fontina, or goat Gouda, grated

2 tablespoons all-purpose flour

1 tablespoon extra-virgin olive oil

2 cloves garlic, minced

6 tablespoons trebbiano or other dry white wine

1/4 teaspoon freshly ground black pepper

8 ounces manouri or fresh chèvre, crumbled

1/4 cup niçoise, kalamata, or other brined black olives, pitted and minced

1/4 cup oil-packed sun-dried tomatoes, drained and minced

2 teaspoons minced fresh oregano leaves

Toss the Comté with the flour in a bowl and set aside. In a fondue pot, heat the oil over medium heat. Add the garlic and cook, stirring frequently, until the garlic is pale golden, about 1 minute. Add the wine and pepper and bring to a boil. Decrease the heat to medium-low and add the Comté mixture, 1/2 cup at a time, stirring until melted after each addition. Add the manouri and stir until smooth, then stir in the olives, tomatoes, and oregano. Serve immediately.

Makes 3 1/2 cups

continued

SERVE WITH: toasted Italian bread or focaccia cubes • Italian olive oil crackers • pita triangles or chips • red bell pepper chunks • fennel strips • canned artichoke hearts

BEVERAGE SUGGESTIONS: sauvignon blanc • dry rosé • trebbiano

CHEESE NOTES: Manouri is a Greek cheese made from sheep's or goat's milk or a combination of the two and is softer, creamier, and less salty than feta. Used in both savory and sweet dishes, manouri is often served for breakfast with just a drizzle of honey; it's also delicious as a base for cheesecake.

Midnight Moon at the Oasis

Our combination of lime vodka, goat's milk Gouda, and harissa—the spicy, slightly smoky North African red pepper paste—may seem to push the boundaries of fusion cuisine. But you'll find that the flavors intertwine as elegantly as threads in a Persian carpet. Though you can make harissa at home, you can also buy excellent versions in tubes or cans at specialty stores (see Resources, page 115) or Middle Eastern groceries. Bay Area distillers Domaine Charbay and Hangar One both make fantastic lime vodkas. Since you need only two tablespoons for the recipe, have fun coming up with ways to use up the rest of the bottle!

1 pound Midnight Moon or other goat Gouda, grated

2 tablespoons all-purpose flour

1 cup albariño or pinot grigio

2 tablespoons lime vodka or freshly squeezed lime juice

2 tablespoons harissa

Freshly ground black pepper

Toss the cheese with the flour in a bowl and set aside. In a fondue pot, bring the wine to a boil over medium-high heat.

Decrease the heat to medium-low and add the cheese mixture, $1/2$ cup at a time, stirring until melted after each addition. Add the vodka and the harissa and stir to combine. Season the fondue with pepper to taste. Serve immediately.

Makes 3 cups

SERVE WITH: toasted pita triangles • roasted lamb, cut into bite-size pieces • cucumber sticks • carrot sticks • toasted sesame seeds

BEVERAGE SUGGESTIONS: dry rosé • syrah or Rhône-style red • wheat beer

CHEESE NOTES: Creamy and nutty with a hint of caramel, Midnight Moon is one of our favorite fondue cheeses. Made from goat's milk by Cypress Grove Chèvre in Humboldt County, California, it shines on its own in a fondue. But we suggest you also try it other ways, layered with intriguing flavors—like on toasted walnut bread with fig jam or quince paste.

Getting Your Goat

Here is our riff on the classic herbed goat cheese theme of the past twenty years. This fondue features a pleasing combination of mild goat cheese, herbs, and black pepper that we think is one of the best things to ever happen to a glass of sauvignon blanc. Laura Chenel is famous for her fresh chèvre, but we also love her aged tome, which is featured in this fondue recipe. If you can't find it, substitute a goat or cow's milk Gouda or Edam.

1 pound Laura Chenel Goat Tome, Gouda, or Edam, rind discarded and grated

2 tablespoons all-purpose flour

1 cup sauvignon blanc or other fruity white wine

$1/2$ cup chopped fresh chives

Freshly ground black pepper

Toss the cheese with the flour in a bowl and set aside. In a fondue pot, bring the wine to a boil over medium-high heat. Decrease the heat to low and add the cheese mixture, $1/2$ cup at a time, stirring until melted after each addition. Stir in the chives and black pepper to taste. Serve immediately.

Makes 3 cups

SERVE WITH: toasted baguette cubes • breadsticks • red or Yukon gold potatoes, roasted or steamed • persimmon chunks (Fuyu, the crunchy variety) • tart apple chunks • toasted breadcrumbs • chopped toasted almonds

BEVERAGE SUGGESTIONS: sauvignon blanc • viognier • blanc de blancs (sparkling wine)

CHEESE NOTES: Not only do goats produce milk that makes great cheese, they're good company and tireless comedians. California produces many excellent goat cheeses, but one of the pioneers of California goat cheese is Laura Chenel, who started her business in Sonoma more than twenty-five years ago. Good quality goat cheese should never have a super-goaty flavor, as this is an indication of poor sanitation at the dairy. Also high quality are the creamy California goat cheeses from Redwood Hill Farm, Goat's Leap, and Cypress Grove.

Melted Makeovers

FAVORITE FOODS AS FONDUE

Cheesy Maple Brunch

When maple-fiend Brigid suggested flavoring this creamy concoction with maple extract, Lenny thought she was off her rocker. Lenny became a believer shortly after dunking a forkful of sausage, pancake, and ripe pear. A great addition to your brunch menu, this fondue complements waffles, English muffins, and pancakes, as well as most breakfast meats and your favorite fruit. Another round of mimosas, anyone?

8 ounces Port Salut, grated

8 ounces mild Cheddar, grated

2 tablespoons all-purpose flour

1 cup whole milk

2 teaspoons maple extract

Toss the cheeses with the flour in a bowl and set aside. In a fondue pot, bring the milk and the maple extract to a boil over medium-high heat. Decrease the heat to low and add the cheese mixture, $1/2$ cup at a time, stirring until melted after each addition. Serve immediately.

Makes 3 cups

SERVE WITH: toasted English muffins, cut into bite-size pieces • waffles or pancakes, cut into bite-size pieces • pear chunks • apple chunks • pineapple chunks • seedless grapes • cooked breakfast sausages, cut into bite-size pieces • ham or Canadian bacon, cut into bite-size cubes

BEVERAGE SUGGESTIONS: mimosas • sparkling wine with a splash of pear or apple brandy • coffee or black tea

CHEESE NOTES: Port Salut, a mild, semi-soft cow's milk cheese with a distinctive orange rind, was first produced in the 1800s in Brittany by French Trappist monks. In 1959, the monks sold the distribution rights to a major French creamery and Port Salut is now widely available in American supermarkets and specialty stores. The orange rind should be removed before grating the cheese for fondue; to do this, peel off what you can with your fingers, then scrape off what remains with the back of a paring knife.

Okey-Dokey Artichokey

Thank goodness our intrepid ancestors had the good sense to figure out how to eat the artichoke. This purple flower with its lethal spines grows on a raggedy grayish-greenish stalk that looks like it's from outer space. Inspired by the popular mayonnaise-o-licious artichoke party dip, this fondue has flavor galore. Artichokes are notoriously tricky to pair with wine, as they tend to make most wines taste sweeter than they are. The Austrian grüner veltliner has a crisp, peppery quality that makes it one of the only reliably artichoke-friendly wines we know. We've tried this recipe unsuccessfully with other crisp white wines, so use grüner veltliner to insure the best flavor. If you have trouble finding it in your area, check out some of our online sources (see Resources, page 115).

1 pound Comté or Fontina

4 ounces Parmigiano-Reggiano

2 tablespoons all-purpose flour

1 tablespoon extra-virgin olive oil

6 cloves garlic, minced

$1/2$ teaspoon red pepper flakes

$1^1/2$ cups grüner veltliner

1 (12-ounce) can marinated artichoke hearts, drained and chopped

Freshly ground black pepper

Toss the cheeses with the flour in a bowl and set aside. In a fondue pot, heat the olive oil over medium-high heat. Add the garlic and pepper flakes and cook, stirring frequently, until the garlic is pale golden, about 1 minute. Add the wine and bring to a boil. Decrease the heat to medium-low and add the cheese mixture, $1/2$ cup at a time, stirring until melted after each addition. Stir in the artichokes, then season with black pepper to taste. Serve immediately.

Makes 4 cups

SERVE WITH: toasted baguette or Italian bread cubes • breadsticks • hearty crackers • cooked, peeled shrimp • red bell pepper chunks • pickled peppers

BEVERAGE SUGGESTIONS: grüner veltliner • wheat beer • pilsner

CHEESE NOTES: Produced in Italy's Emilia-Romagna region since the Middle Ages, Parmigiano-Reggiano can be made only from the milk of grass-fed cows between May 1 and November 11. Whey left over in the cheesemaking process has traditionally been used as feed for the pigs from which Parma hams (Prosciutto) are produced.

Philly's Phave

The Philly cheesesteak debate rages on: Pat's or Geno's? American, provolone, or Cheez Whiz? "Wit'" or "Wit'-out"? So many choices—we just decided to throw it all in a pot and let our barbarian party guests work it out. This departure from tradition should have both cheesesteak and fondue purists up in arms, but they won't be able to resist its cheesy charm. If you want to go a little more traditional, try it with American Cheddar or provolone in place of the stinky European varieties used here.

8 ounces each raclette and Emmental, or 16 ounces Cheddar or provolone, grated

2 tablespoons olive oil

6 green onions, white and light green parts only, minced

1 onion, diced

1 green bell pepper, diced

2 cups coarsely chopped mushrooms

Kosher salt and freshly ground black pepper

2 tablespoons all-purpose flour

1 1/2 cups beef stock

Toss the cheeses together in a bowl and set aside. In a fondue pot, heat the oil over medium-high heat. Add the green onions, onion, bell pepper, and mushrooms and cook, stirring, until slightly softened, about 5 to 8 minutes. Season with salt and pepper to taste and add the flour. Cook, stirring frequently, until all the moisture is gone from the mushrooms, 4 to 5 minutes. Add the beef stock and stir until the mixture comes to a boil. Decrease the heat to medium-low and add the cheese mixture, 1/2 cup at a time, stirring until melted after each addition. Serve immediately.

Makes about 4 cups

SERVE WITH: toasted Italian or French bread cubes • cooked beef steak or roast, cut into bite-size cubes (great for leftover prime rib) • assorted pickles • cooked Italian sausages, cut into bite-size pieces

BEVERAGE SUGGESTIONS: beer • root beer • more beer

CHEESE NOTES: All Emmental is Swiss cheese, but not all Swiss cheese is Emmental. Originally made in Bern canton's Emme valley, Emmental is not a protected regional name and so you will also find Emmental cheese made in Scandinavia and Germany. Firm, yellow, and mildly piquant, Emmental's large open holes are created by carbon dioxide released as the active bacteria consume the milk's lactic acid.

Reuben, Rearranged

The path to Lenny's heart is paved with Reuben sandwiches. That tangy, salty, cheesy deli favorite inspired this hearty fondue, which can warm your guests on a chilly fall evening or at a tailgate party. You can use all Swiss cheese, or a combination of Swiss and Gouda.

1 tablespoon olive oil

1 tablespoon caraway seed

1 small red onion, diced

1$^{1}/_{2}$ cups sauerkraut, minced

2 tablespoons all-purpose flour

1$^{1}/_{2}$ cups beer

16 ounces Swiss or Gouda or a blend, grated

4 teaspoons cider vinegar

Kosher salt and freshly ground black pepper

In a fondue pot, heat the oil over medium-high heat. Add the caraway seed and cook, stirring frequently, for 1 minute. Add the onion, sauerkraut, and flour and cook, stirring, until the onion is soft, about 5 to 8 minutes. Add the beer and bring to a boil. Decrease the heat to medium-low, so that the mixture simmers gently. Add the cheese, $^{1}/_{2}$ cup at a time, stirring until melted after each addition. Add the vinegar and stir until smooth, then season with salt and pepper to taste. Serve immediately.

Makes 3 cups

SERVE WITH: toasted rye bread cubes • pastrami and corned beef, cut into bite-size cubes • red or Yukon gold potatoes, roasted or steamed • Russian or Thousand Island dressing • assorted pickles

BEVERAGE SUGGESTIONS: Crémant d'Alsace (sparkling wine) • lager or pilsner • dry riesling

CHEESE NOTES: Holey cow! The term "Swiss cheese" refers to any of a number of cheeses like Emmental that are firm, yellow, and dense in texture, with the distinctive look of being riddled with holes. The bacteria that produce the hole-forming gases as the cheese ages also contribute to its flavor development; generally, the larger the eyes in a Swiss cheese, the more pronounced its flavor.

Queso Mi Mucho

We felt obligated to fondue-deconstruct the quesadilla, one of our favorite no-time-to-cook meals. Serve this fondue with just a stack of warm tortillas to a crowd of your busy friends and see how quickly it vanishes. Latin ingredients, from chiles to cheeses, have become much easier to find, so look for traditional Hispanic cheeses at your local Latin grocery, specialty market, or well-stocked supermarket. For our fondue, we used queso quesadilla, as it has the best melted texture of any we tried, but you can also look for queso Oaxaca and queso asadero. Be sure not to use fresh cheeses such as panela and queso blanco for fondue, because they are meant to maintain their texture when heated and will not melt properly.

2 teaspoons cumin seed

1 cup dry, fruity white wine

1 pound queso quesadilla or jack cheese, cut into small pieces

6 canned chipotle chiles in adobo, minced

2 tablespoons tequila

Juice of 1/2 lime, or more as desired

Heat a fondue pot over medium-high heat. Add the cumin seed, stirring frequently until it darkens slightly and smells toasty, about 1 to 2 minutes. Add the wine and bring to a boil. Decrease the heat to medium-low and add the cheese, 1/2 cup at a time, stirring until melted after each addition. Add the chiles, tequila, and lime juice and stir until smooth. Add more lime juice to taste, if desired. Serve immediately.

Makes 3 cups

SERVE WITH: tortilla chips • flour and corn tortillas heated on a griddle or frying pan • grilled chicken, cut into bite-size pieces • grilled zucchini or summer squash, cut into bite-size pieces • radishes • chopped toasted pumpkin seeds

BEVERAGE SUGGESTIONS: ale or lager • dry or off-dry riesling • chardonnay

CHEESE NOTES: Smooth, soft, mild, and white, queso quesadilla is a favorite Mexican melting and snacking cheese, as well as the key ingredient to the traditional Mexican fondue dish, queso fundido.

Combination Pizza Fondue

A spicy cauldron of pizza goodness. Experiment with your own favorite toppings and be creative. If you're feeling conservative, you can leave out all the veggies and have a delicious cheese-pizza fondue.

8 ounces Fontina, grated

6 ounces mozzarella, grated

2 ounces Parmigiano-Reggiano, grated

2 tablespoons olive oil

1 onion, diced

4 cloves garlic, minced

1 small green bell pepper, diced

Kosher salt and freshly ground black pepper

2 tablespoons all-purpose flour

2 cups coarsely chopped mushrooms

1 (14.5-ounce) can diced tomatoes, drained and liquid reserved

1 (4.5-ounce) can minced black olives

1 teaspoon red pepper flakes

2 tablespoons fresh oregano or a combination of fresh oregano and fresh thyme, minced

$1/2$ cup pinot grigio or other dry white wine

Combine the cheeses in a bowl and set aside. In a fondue pot, heat the oil over medium-high heat. Add the onion, garlic, and bell pepper and cook, stirring frequently, until softened, about 2 minutes. Season with salt and pepper and add the flour, stirring to coat the vegetables. Add the mushrooms and cook, stirring frequently, until most of the moisture has evaporated, 2 to 3 minutes. Add the drained tomatoes, olives, pepper flakes, and oregano and cook, stirring frequently, 2 minutes. Add the wine and $1/2$ cup of the reserved tomato liquid and bring to a boil, stirring occasionally. Decrease the heat to medium-low, so that the mixture simmers gently. Add the cheese mixture, $1/2$ cup at a time, stirring until melted after each addition. Serve immediately.

Makes $3^{1}/2$ cups

SERVE WITH: toasted Italian bread and focaccia cubes • crisp breadsticks • cooked Italian sausages, cut into bite-size pieces • thick slices of pepperoni • cherry tomatoes

BEVERAGE SUGGESTIONS: ale or lager • dry rosé • tempranillo

CHEESE NOTES: Three of Italy's best known cheeses, mozzarella, Fontina, and Parmigiano-Reggiano, represent the diversity of Italian cheese-making styles. Milky, mild mozzarella is a stretchy wonder when melted and serves as the perfect flavor backdrop for salty and tart pizza toppings. Rich, nutty fontina combines well with other cheeses but also makes one of the best grilled cheese sandwiches you'll ever have. And you really haven't experienced Italian cheese until you've grated a mountain of the sublimely savory Parmigiano-Reggiano atop your favorite pasta dish; this cheese is worth the wait for its two years of aging!

Big Bacony Blue

Pizza Azzurro, a fabulous pizzeria in Napa, California, serves one of the best salads around: a huge wedge of iceberg lettuce doused with creamy blue cheese dressing and scattered with thick bacon chunks and radishes. We thought this salty, flavorful salad with its special iceberg crunch would also make a swell fondue. Though you can use any creamy blue cheese, we recommend Pt. Reyes Original Blue, made in Marin County, California. Its smooth texture and distinct flavor stand up to the salty bacon and anything you might want to dip in it.

8 tablespoons whole milk or half-and-half

2 teaspoons cornstarch

4 slices thick-cut bacon, diced

12 ounces Pt. Reyes Original Blue, crumbled

Combine 1 tablespoon of the milk and the cornstarch in a small bowl and set aside. Heat a fondue pot over medium-high heat and add the bacon. Cook, stirring frequently, until the bacon is crisp, about 8 to 12 minutes, depending on the bacon's thickness. Pour off the excess fat and discard or save for another use. Return the pot to the heat and add the remaining milk. Bring to a boil, then decrease the heat to medium-low and add the cheese and the cornstarch mixture. Cook, stirring frequently, until the cheese is completely melted and the fondue thickens slightly (it will be rather thin). Serve immediately.

Makes 2 cups

continued

SERVE WITH: toasted bread cubes • cherry tomatoes • cucumber sticks • radishes • romaine hearts or chunks of iceberg lettuce • apple chunks • pear chunks • fresh figs, quartered

BEVERAGE SUGGESTIONS: chenin blanc • ice wine or late-harvest riesling • fruity sauvignon blanc (light or no oak)

CHEESE NOTES: Most likely, the method for making blue cheese was discovered by accident in caves used for aging cheese. First, the cheese is inoculated with the *Penicillium roqueforti* mold. Then, it's punctured all over to create tiny air holes that will encourage the mold to grow inside the cheese. Depending on the type of blue cheese (Gorgonzola, Stilton, and so on), the mold will be introduced at various stages of the cheesemaking process. Blue cheese can be made from sheep's, cow's, or goat's milk and is delicious with fruit and in salads.

Hawaii 5-Oh

After we created the pièce de résistance Combination Pizza Fondue, we contemplated other pizza classics and how they would translate to the fondue format. Though Brigid's never been a fan of the Hawaiian pizza, she became a convert after Lenny created this salty, smoky, sweet fondue delight. It is particularly addictive with fresh pineapple and dates. Use a good-quality smoked Cheddar, as some of the waxier smoked Goudas, though easier to find, don't melt very well and lend a funny texture.

1 pound smoked Cheddar, grated

2 tablespoons all-purpose flour

2 tablespoons canola or vegetable oil

4 ounces smoked Canadian bacon, minced

1/2 cup sparkling apple cider

Toss the cheese with the flour in a bowl and set aside. In a fondue pot, heat the oil over medium-high heat. Add the Canadian bacon and cook, stirring frequently, until lightly browned, about 5 minutes. Add the cider and bring to a boil. Decrease the heat to medium-low and add the cheese mixture, 1/2 cup at a time, stirring until melted after each addition. Serve immediately.

Makes 3 cups

SERVE WITH: cherry tomatoes • pineapple chunks • pitted dates • toasted focaccia or Italian bread cubes • breadsticks

BEVERAGE SUGGESTIONS: off-dry rosé • chardonnay • hard apple or pear cider

CHEESE NOTES: Smoked Cheddar gives this fondue an extra kick of smoky goodness that balances so nicely with sweet, juicy pineapple. Look for good quality aged smoked Cheddars from Vermont's Shelburne Farms and Grafton Village and Oregon's Tillamook.

Queso con Chili

We dream of a world in which chili dogs are served at every meal. Okay, maybe it would get old, but girls can dream, right? If you're feeling ambitious, make your own chili for this fondue. Or freeze a pint next time you make a big pot and all you have to do is defrost. This fondue is perfect for a Super Bowl or Final Four party. Having made it for both occasions, we recommend doubling the recipe since it tends to go fast. Masa harina is a finely ground cornmeal used in Mexican and Central American cooking. Look for it in the Latin section of your grocery store or specialty store.

1 pound mild Cheddar or Monterey Jack or a blend

2 tablespoons masa harina

2 canned chipotle chiles in adobo, minced

1 cup beer

1 tablespoon chili powder

2 teaspoons ground cumin

1 teaspoon dried oregano

1 (15-ounce) can chili, any style, or 2 cups homemade chili

Toss the cheese with the masa harina in a bowl and set aside. In a fondue pot, combine the chipotles, beer, chili powder, cumin, and oregano and bring to a boil over medium-high heat, stirring occasionally. Decrease the heat to medium-low and simmer for 5 minutes. Add the cheese mixture, $1/2$ cup at a time, stirring to melt after each addition. Add the chili and stir to combine. Continue to cook, stirring frequently, until the fondue is heated through. Serve immediately.

Makes 5 cups

SERVE WITH: cocktail wieners or hot dogs, cut into bite-size pieces • toasted corn bread cubes • finely minced green onions or red onions • tortilla chips • celery sticks • jicama sticks

BEVERAGE SUGGESTIONS: lager or ale • margaritas on the rocks • syrah/shiraz

CHEESE NOTES: Originally made in the 1800s by Spanish Franciscan monks in Monterey, California, Monterey cheese became "jack cheese" when Scottish-born California land baron David Jacks expanded commercial production of the cheese and marketed it under the name "Monterey Jack."

Curried Lambchopper

Lenny has the good fortune to be married to Chris, a chef of Guyanese-Indian heritage. Not only a stand-up guy and great cook, Chris knows a thing or two about curry. Lenny has grown to love the delightful and complex flavors of Indian cuisine. You won't, of course, find fondue in any traditional Indian kitchen. But we surprised ourselves with how well the Indian spice mixture married with the mildly tangy richness of Lambchopper, a mild sheep's milk cheese. Enjoy this decidedly nontraditional fondue with your favorite vegetables for curry like cauliflower, broccoli, and potatoes.

2 tablespoons unsalted butter

1 onion, diced

2 tablespoons Madras curry powder

1 cup off-dry riesling

1 pound Lambchopper or other semi-soft Gouda-style cheese, grated

In a fondue pot, melt the butter over high heat, then decrease the heat to medium. Add the onion and cook until golden, 4 to 5 minutes. Add the curry powder and stir to coat the onion, then add the wine and bring to a boil. Decrease the heat to medium-low and add the cheese, $1/2$ cup at a time, stirring until melted after each addition. Serve immediately.

Makes 3 cups

SERVE WITH: steamed cauliflower florets • steamed broccoli florets • red or Yukon gold potatoes, roasted or boiled • red bell pepper chunks • naan or other Indian flatbreads, cut into bite-size pieces • chopped toasted almonds • chopped raisins • minced green onions • toasted unsweetened coconut flakes

BEVERAGE SUGGESTIONS: riesling • off-dry rosé • gewürztraminer

CHEESE NOTES: Lambchopper is an organic sheep's milk Gouda made in Holland for the California cheese company Cypress Grove. Its mild but distinct flavor is worth seeking out for this fondue, but if you can't find it, use any semi-soft Gouda.

No "Drac" Jack

Add the rich, mellow flavor of slow-roasted garlic to your fondue—you'll win rave reviews from your guests—and no chance of Dracula showing up to spoil the party!

3 small or 2 large heads garlic

1/4 cup olive oil

1/2 teaspoon kosher salt

1/4 teaspoon freshly ground black pepper

1 cup beer

1 pound Monterey or Sonoma jack, grated

2 tablespoons all-purpose flour

2 teaspoons minced fresh thyme leaves

Preheat the oven to 350°F. Remove the loose, papery outside skin from the garlic heads and trim 1/2 inch off the tops. Place the heads in a shallow baking dish, cut side up, and cover with the olive oil, salt, and pepper. Cover tightly with aluminum foil and bake until very soft, about 1 hour and 15 minutes. Allow the garlic to cool, still covered, to room temperature. When cool, squeeze each head from the root end to force out the garlic cloves directly into the fondue pot. Mash the cloves with a fork into a semi-smooth paste. Add the beer and whisk to combine.

Toss the cheese with the flour in a bowl and set aside. Bring the beer mixture to a boil over medium-high heat. Decrease the heat to medium-low and add the cheese mixture, 1/2 cup at a time, stirring until melted after each addition. Stir in the thyme. Serve immediately.

Makes 3 cups

SERVE WITH: steamed cauliflower florets • steamed broccoli florets • toasted sourdough bread and focaccia cubes • cherry tomatoes • roasted red or Yukon gold potatoes • cooked sausages, cut into bite-size pieces

BEVERAGE SUGGESTIONS: California chardonnay • blanc de blancs (sparkling wine) • sangiovese

CHEESE NOTES: In the late 1800s, Spanish monks in Monterey achieved cheesemaking success with a new American cheese that would be called "jack." A few years later, Italian cheesemakers just up the coast in Sonoma came up with their own delicious version. Today, Sonoma and Monterey jack cheeses live in harmony in cheese shops and restaurants across the country.

Pimiento Cheese Perfection

When our friends Ben and Karen Barker, who own the Magnolia Grill in Durham, North Carolina, learned we were doing a fondue book, they both said: "You've gotta do pimiento cheese!" A true Southern classic, pimiento cheese can be found gracing celery sticks and white bread at picnics, potlucks, and family reunions around the South. Pimiento cheese is always made with orange Cheddar, so if you seek authenticity, steer clear of the more elegant white types. As a spread, pimiento cheese is bound by mayonnaise; we've based the fondue version on another traditional health food—beer.

1 pound sharp orange Cheddar, grated

$1/2$ teaspoon dry mustard

2 tablespoons all-purpose flour

2 cloves garlic, halved lengthwise

1 cup beer

2 tablespoons cream sherry

1 (4-ounce) jar diced pimientos, drained

1 tablespoon Worcestershire sauce

$1/2$ teaspoon Tabasco sauce

1 teaspoon kosher salt

Freshly ground black pepper

Toss the cheese, mustard, and flour together in a bowl and set aside. Rub the inside of a fondue pot with the cut sides of the garlic, then place the pieces in the pot. Add the beer and sherry and bring to a simmer over medium-high heat. Decrease the heat to medium-low and simmer 3 to 4 minutes. Add the cheese mixture, $1/2$ cup at a time, stirring until melted after each addition. Add the pimientos, Worcestershire, and Tabasco and stir until combined. Season with the salt and pepper to taste. Serve immediately.

Makes 3 cups

continued

SERVE WITH: toasted white bread cubes •
Ritz or your favorite variety of crackers •
celery sticks • pickled okra

BEVERAGE SUGGESTIONS: dry rosé • ale
or lager • Rioja

CHEESE NOTES: Though Cheddar-style cheese is produced in many countries around the world, it originated in the town of Cheddar, in Southwest England. Much Cheddar cheese is mass-produced and its quality varies greatly. But now widely available in the United States are excellent English and American farmstead Cheddars that are still made with traditional methods. White Cheddar versus orange? The only difference is the addition of a natural food coloring from the achiote tree, annatto, a custom that was probably introduced to achieve a consistent color from batch to batch.

Whiskey Tango Game Day

At Lenny's childhood home in Oklahoma, if the Sooners were playing on college-football Saturdays, the Velveeta was melting. Game day wasn't complete without a pot of good ole orange American ingenuity. With this fondue, Lenny continues the tradition that her mom, Dixie, began with the recipe from the side of the Velveeta box. And the name? If you're familiar with the military radio alphabet, you'll probably be able to figure out how we came up with it!

2 tablespoons olive oil

8 ounces ground beef or pork

6 green onions, white and light green parts only, minced, or $1/2$ cup canned mild green chiles

1 onion, diced

1 cup canned diced tomatoes, undrained

4 canned chipotle chiles in adobo, minced

1 pound processed cheese product (like Velveeta), grated

Kosher salt and freshly ground black pepper

In a fondue pot, heat the oil over medium-high heat. Add the beef and cook, stirring occasionally, until brown, 8 to 10 minutes.

Add the green onions and the onion and cook, stirring occasionally, until they are soft, about 5 to 7 minutes, then drain off any excess fat and discard. Add the tomatoes with their liquid and the chipotles and bring to a boil. Decrease the heat to medium-low and add the cheese, $1/2$ cup at a time, stirring until melted after each addition. Season with salt and pepper to taste. Serve immediately.

Makes 4 cups

SERVE WITH: toasted white bread cubes • tortilla chips • celery sticks • cocktail wieners • Ritz or your favorite variety of crackers

BEVERAGE SUGGESTIONS: Dr. Pepper • beer (Bud Light) • RC Cola

CHEESE NOTES: A true American classic, Velveeta was actually created by Swiss immigrant cheesemaker Emil Frey in 1918. Whey, a cheesemaking by-product, gives Velveeta its characteristic moist, rubbery texture and makes it a very cost-effective cheese to produce. Its cheery orange glow is a comfort in countless American homes.

How Sweet It Is

SWEET FONDUE FINALES

Lemon with a Twist

This is the perfect accompaniment for all your summer fruit favorites: berries, peaches, cherries—you name it. It is also the ideal devilish dip for angel food cake. For a slightly more exotic flavor, try Meyer lemon zest, or get really wild and use tangerine zest instead of lemon and Cointreau instead of limoncello—delicious!

1¼ pounds white chocolate (such as Callebaut, El Rey, or Lindt), chopped

1¼ cups heavy cream

3 tablespoons grated lemon zest (from about 4 lemons)

1 teaspoon lemon extract, plus more as needed

2 tablespoons limoncello (lemon liqueur), plus more as needed

Place the chocolate in a heatproof bowl and set aside. In a heavy saucepan, combine the cream and zest. Bring to a boil over high heat and remove from heat. Let sit 15 minutes to allow the zest to infuse the cream. Pour the cream mixture through a fine mesh strainer into a clean heavy saucepan and discard the zest. Reheat over medium-high heat until just below a boil, then pour over the chocolate. Allow the chocolate mixture to sit 5 minutes, then whisk gently until smooth and the chocolate is completely melted. Whisk in the lemon extract and limoncello, adding more of both to taste if desired. Transfer immediately to a fondue pot and serve.

Makes 4 cups

SERVE WITH: blueberries and blackberries • strawberry halves • peach slices • plum slices • pitted sweet cherries • toasted angel food cake cubes

BEVERAGE SUGGESTIONS: late harvest riesling • Moscato d'Asti • pomegranate mimosa

Yo Ho Ho and Some Coconut Rum

Something about growing up in Idaho's hot, arid summers and snowy winters must have given Brigid a taste for the tropics. Passion fruit, coconut, pineapple, you name it—if it grows near the equator, on an island, or on a palm tree, she'll turn it into a dessert. This fondue leads a double life: one as a tropical temptress, luring unsuspecting pineapple and mango chunks to their demise with its rum-laced coconut creaminess; the other as the girl next door, charming chunks of cake into a swingin' German-chocolate hot tub party.

1 cup sweetened flaked coconut

1 cup heavy cream

1 pound white chocolate, chopped

2 tablespoons coconut or dark rum

Preheat the oven to 350°F. Spread the coconut on a baking sheet, place it in the oven, and toast until light brown, 10 to 12 minutes, stirring every 5 minutes to color evenly. Allow it to cool, then transfer to a heavy saucepan and add the cream. Bring the cream to a boil over medium-high heat, then remove from heat. Allow the cream mixture to steep 10 minutes. Place the chocolate in a heatproof bowl and cover with the cream mixture. With a wooden spoon or rubber spatula, stir the chocolate mixture until smooth and uniform. If the chocolate does not melt completely, set the bowl on top of a pot of barely simmering water and heat, stirring constantly, until the chocolate is melted and mixture is smooth. Add the rum and stir until smooth. Transfer immediately to a fondue pot and serve.

Makes 3 cups

SERVE WITH: pineapple chunks • mango chunks • papaya chunks • strawberries • chopped toasted macadamia nuts • chopped toasted pecans • devil's food pound cake cubes (page 111)

BEVERAGE SUGGESTIONS: late-harvest gewürztraminer • Muscat de Baumes-de-Venise • ice wine

Chocolate Raspberry

Brigid first experienced this elegant flavor combination in the early 1970s at the candy counter of the "opulent" Idaho Falls Sears store. There, she found delectable fruit jelly sticks enrobed in dark chocolate. Pastry chefs at upscale restaurants in the late 1980s must have had similar childhood experiences (or just good sense); chocolate and raspberry proliferated on dessert menus everywhere. A classic combination, this fondue is a tribute to sweet memories of old-school Sears candy counters.

12 ounces semisweet chocolate, chopped

1/2 cup seedless raspberry jam

1/4 cup framboise or other raspberry liqueur

1 cup heavy cream

Place the chocolate in a heatproof bowl and set aside. In a small, heavy saucepan, combine the jam and the framboise, breaking up any large jam chunks with a fork. Cook the jam mixture over medium-low heat, stirring occasionally, until the jam has completely melted. Remove the pan from the heat and set aside. In a separate heavy saucepan, bring the cream to a boil over medium-high heat. Immediately pour the cream and the jam mixture over the chocolate and allow it to sit 5 minutes before whisking until the chocolate is completely melted. Transfer immediately to a fondue pot and serve.

Makes 3 cups

SERVE WITH: sour cream pound cake cubes (page 112) • shortbread cookies • banana chunks • pear chunks • crystallized ginger chunks • candied orange peel • chopped toasted almonds or hazelnuts • toasted flaked sweetened or unsweetened coconut

BEVERAGE SUGGESTIONS: late-harvest zinfandel or shiraz • Kir Royale (sparkling wine and crème de cassis) • ruby port

Mexican Chocolate

Artisan chocolate is now all the rage, and you can find dozens of great quality brands at your grocery store and specialty shops. You can make this fondue with all bitter-sweet or all milk chocolate, or any combination of the two—experiment with different styles and discover your favorite. For a nice dipping variety, purchase an assortment of *pan dulce* and other Mexican sweet breads at a good Latino market. You can also opt for store-bought marshmallows, but our homemade mango ones are worth the extra effort and can be made a day or more before you plan to serve them.

9 ounces milk chocolate, chopped

3 ounces bittersweet or semisweet chocolate, chopped

1 1/2 cups heavy cream

4 or 5 cinnamon sticks

1/8 to 1/4 teaspoon red pepper flakes

1/2 teaspoon vanilla extract

2 tablespoons Kahlúa or other coffee liqueur

Place the chocolates in a large heatproof bowl and set aside. In a heavy saucepan, combine the cream, cinnamon sticks, and 1/8 to 1/4 teaspoon of the pepper flakes (the amount depends on how spicy you want the fondue). Bring to a boil over medium-high heat. Remove the pan from the heat and allow it to sit 20 minutes so the flavors can infuse the cream. Strain the cream mixture through a fine mesh strainer and discard the cinnamon and pepper flakes. Return the cream to the saucepan and bring it to a boil again over medium-high heat. Remove the pan from the heat and pour the cream over the chopped chocolate. Let the mixture sit for several minutes, then whisk gently until smooth and the chocolate is completely melted. Whisk in the vanilla and liqueur. Transfer immediately to a fondue pot and serve.

Makes 2 cups

SERVE WITH: plain or mango marshmallows (page 113) • Mexican *pan dulce* and churros • strawberry halves • pineapple chunks • mango chunks • toasted chopped almonds • toasted flaked sweetened or unsweetened coconut

BEVERAGE SUGGESTIONS: tawny port • California pinot noir (fruity style) • black muscat

Ode to a Candy Bar

Admission is the first step: Brigid is a Snickers junkie. A Snickers bar makes a clear case for the whole being greater than the sum of the parts. It leaves no taste bud lonely, no craving unsatisfied. Inspired by the genius of Snickers, Brigid created a fondue that satisfies multiple cravings. You can use crunchy or smooth peanut butter, but the natural style, oil-on-top stuff doesn't work; go for the hydrogenated, emulsified brands like Jif or Skippy. We also recommend semisweet rather than bittersweet chocolate to allow the peanut butter and caramel flavors to shine through.

1 cup crunchy or smooth salted peanut butter (not natural-style)

1 1/2 cups granulated sugar

1/2 cup water

2 teaspoons light corn syrup

2 cups heavy cream

3 ounces semisweet chocolate, chopped

1 teaspoon vanilla extract

Place the peanut butter in a large, heat-proof bowl and set aside. In a deep, heavy saucepan (one with a light interior so you can see the color of the sugar as it cooks), combine the sugar, water, and corn syrup. Cover and bring to a boil over medium-high heat. Remove the cover and cook the sugar without stirring until it starts to turn golden around the edges, 5 to 8 minutes. Swirl the pan as necessary to ensure even cooking. When the sugar is deep amber, add the cream—be careful, the mixture will bubble up and steam. Stir the caramel until it is uniform and all the sugar has dissolved, returning it to the heat if necessary to completely melt any lumps. Remove the pan from the heat and pour the caramel over the peanut butter, whisking until smooth. Add the chopped chocolate and vanilla and whisk until the mixture is smooth and the chocolate is completely melted. Immediately transfer the mixture to a fondue pot and serve, or allow to cool to room temperature before transferring to a storage container. The fondue can be made up to 2 days ahead and stored in the refrigerator. To serve, reheat in a saucepan over medium-low heat, stirring frequently, until fluid.

Makes 4 cups

SERVE WITH: shortbread cookies • peanut butter Rice Krispies treats • marshmallows • Graham crackers • banana chunks • Granny Smith apple chunks • chopped toasted salted peanuts

BEVERAGE SUGGESTIONS: Diet Coke • tawny port • cream sherry

Chocolate Hazelnut with Frangelico

Where were you when you discovered Nutella? That post-college backpacking trip to Europe was not complete without having eaten Nutella for at least three meals. It's hard to describe what makes the combination of chocolate, hazelnuts, and sugar so intensely satisfying. But it's that synthesis that we've tried to recreate with this fondue. We recommend a semisweet chocolate (50 to 60 percent cacao), like Valrhona Caraque or Callebaut Semisweet. Try to find a chocolate with nutty undertones, rather than fruity or winey flavors that can compete with the hazelnut. If you can't find hazelnut butter in your local natural foods store or specialty grocery, we list several online sources for it in Resources (see page 115).

10 ounces semisweet chocolate, chopped

1 cup hazelnut butter (unsalted)

1¼ cups heavy cream

1 teaspoon kosher salt

¾ cup granulated sugar

¼ cup Frangelico or other hazelnut liqueur

Place the chocolate and hazelnut butter in a large heatproof bowl and set aside. In a heavy saucepan, combine the cream, salt, and sugar and bring to a boil over high heat. Remove from the heat and pour over the chocolate mixture. Let the mixture sit for several minutes, then whisk gently until smooth and the chocolate is completely melted. Whisk in the liqueur, then pass the mixture through a fine mesh strainer. Transfer immediately to fondue pot and serve.

Makes 4 cups

SERVE WITH: toasted baguette cubes • marshmallows • banana chunks • strawberries • shortbread cookies • marble cake or sour cream pound cake cubes (page 112) • chopped toasted hazelnuts

BEVERAGE SUGGESTIONS: Malmsey Madeira • black muscat • Marsala

Dulce de Leche

Some of us have been known to eat a whole pint of dulce de leche ice cream in a single sitting, so addictive is this South American milk caramel. Just like Ricky Martin, this rich and *suave* Latin import will have you swooning with every dip. Though the recipe has only one ingredient, it's a bit of a time investment; plan your day accordingly so you can attend to the simmering pot. This fondue is extra sweet, so it is best served with tart, slightly acidic fruits, such as pineapple and strawberries. But feel free to experiment with your favorites.

3 (14-ounce) cans sweetened
    condensed milk

With the tip of a bottle opener, pierce the top of each can to make a small hole. Wrap the top of each can tightly with aluminum foil. Place the cans in a deep, heavy saucepan and add enough water so that the cans are immersed to within 1 inch of their tops. Bring the water to a boil over medium-high heat. Reduce the heat so that it just simmers gently (the cans will bounce around a bit, but the water must bubble gently to properly cook the milk). Simmer the cans for 4 hours, adding hot water as needed to maintain the desired water level throughout cooking. After 4 hours, remove the cans from the water, discard the foil, and let cool 15 minutes. Fully remove the can tops with a can opener and scoop the dulce de leche from the cans into a bowl. Whisk the sauce vigorously until it is uniform in texture and color. Immediately transfer to a fondue pot and serve, or cool to room temperature before covering the bowl tightly and storing in the refrigerator until needed. Dulce de leche will keep for several weeks in the refrigerator.

Makes 4 cups

SERVE WITH: strawberries • tart apple chunks (such as Granny Smith) • peach chunks • pineapple chunks • shortbread cookies • devil's food pound cake cubes (page 111) • chopped toasted brazil nuts or cashews

BEVERAGE SUGGESTIONS: late-harvest riesling • Moscato d'Asti • vin santo

From the Malt Shop

Malt is just one of those flavors that drives us wild. A milkshake is just milk and ice cream, but a malt is *magic*. Add a little magic to your fondue experience with this decadent, yet comforting, fondue. Be sure to use a high quality milk chocolate that is flavorful and creamy. Our favorite is Callebaut, but Trader Joe's sells a delicious milk chocolate bar that is also an excellent value.

12 ounces milk chocolate, chopped

2 ounces bittersweet chocolate, chopped

1 1/2 cups heavy cream

3/4 cup malt powder (such as Horlick's or Carnation)

1/4 teaspoon kosher salt

2 tablespoons Irish cream liqueur

Combine the milk and bittersweet chocolates in a large heatproof bowl and set aside. In a heavy saucepan, heat the cream to a boil over high heat. Remove from the heat and whisk in the malt powder and salt. Pour the cream mixture over the chocolate and allow it to sit 5 minutes, then whisk until smooth and the chocolate is completely melted. Whisk in the liqueur. Transfer immediately to a fondue pot and serve.

Makes 3 cups

SERVE WITH: regular or peanut butter Rice Krispy treats • Graham crackers • pecan sandies • banana chunks • strawberries

BEVERAGE SUGGESTIONS: Malmsey Madeira • orange muscat • oloroso sherry

Caramel Latte

Coffee and doughnuts have never been so decadent. This is a rich, creamy coffee-caramel fondue with the bonus of making your own sweet little cinnamon puffs for dipping. Add some bananas and you nearly have all the food groups.

1¼ cups heavy cream

3 tablespoons instant espresso powder

1½ cups sugar

½ cup water

2 teaspoons light corn syrup

In a heavy saucepan, bring the cream to a boil over medium-high heat. Remove from the heat and whisk in the espresso powder until it dissolves completely. In a separate deep, heavy saucepan (one with a light interior so you can see the color of the sugar as it cooks), combine the sugar, water, and corn syrup, stirring until the consistency of wet sand. Cover and bring to a boil over medium-high heat. Remove the cover and cook the sugar without stirring until it starts to turn golden around the edges, 5 to 8 minutes. Swirl the pan as necessary to ensure even cooking.

When the sugar is deep amber, add the cream mixture—be careful, the mixture will bubble up and steam. Stir the caramel until it is uniform and all the sugar has dissolved, returning it to the heat if necessary to completely melt any lumps. Remove the pan from the heat and transfer the caramel to a fondue pot. Allow the caramel to cool slightly before setting the fondue pot on its heat source to serve.

Makes 3 cups

SERVE WITH: cinnamon sugar doughnut holes (page 109) or other purchased doughnuts • banana chunks • pear chunks • cubes of devil's food pound cake (page 111) or other dense chocolate cake • chopped toasted hazelnuts, pecans, or almonds

BEVERAGE SUGGESTIONS: ice wine • oloroso sherry • Malmsey Madeira

Pineapple Upside-Down

Nothing beats the combination of caramel, pineapple, and rich, buttery cake, especially if there's a little rum thrown in for kicks. Don't skimp on the rum—a dark, flavorful Caribbean rum like Gosling's or Appleton Estate will add flavor and dimension, rather than just burning sinuses. When cooking the caramel, keep a plain white plate nearby to check the color. As the caramel cooks, drizzle a little of it onto the plate—it should be deep amber, not golden or brown. It takes a little practice to get it right, but the rich caramel flavor will be your reward.

1¼ cups heavy cream

1½ cups sugar

½ cup water

2 teaspoons light corn syrup

2 to 3 tablespoons dark rum

1 teaspoon vanilla extract

In a heavy saucepan, bring the cream to a boil over medium-high heat and remove it from the heat. In a separate deep, heavy saucepan (one with a light interior so you can see the color of the sugar as it cooks), combine the sugar, water, and corn syrup. Cover and bring to a boil over medium-high heat. Remove the cover and cook the sugar without stirring until it starts to turn golden around the edges, 5 to 8 minutes. Swirl the pan as necessary to ensure even cooking. When the sugar is deep amber, add the cream—be careful, the mixture will bubble up and steam. Stir the caramel until it is uniform and all the sugar has dissolved, returning it to the heat if necessary to completely melt any lumps. Remove the pan from the heat and stir in the rum and vanilla. Immediately transfer the caramel to a fondue pot and serve, or cool to room temperature before transferring to a storage container.

The fondue can be made up to 2 days ahead. To serve, reheat in a saucepan over medium-low heat, stirring frequently, until fluid.

Makes 3 cups

SERVE WITH: sour cream pound cake (page 112) • pineapple chunks • pitted fresh sweet cherries • maraschino or preserved amarena cherries (see Resources, page 115) • chopped toasted pecans

BEVERAGE SUGGESTIONS: demi-sec sparkling wine • muscat canelli • Dark and Stormy cocktail (ginger beer and dark rum)

La Dolce Vita

Creamy and extravagant, a triple-crème cheese such as the French Saint-André or Mt.Tam from California's Cowgirl Creamery served with fruit can be a simple, sophisticated dessert. Add a touch of honey, anise seed, and a splash of vin santo and you've got a fondue fit for a king. A Tuscan dessert wine made from grapes that are dried on straw mats to concentrate their sweetness and flavor, vin santo is traditionally served with biscotti, but it also has a special affinity for rich fall fruits such as pears and figs. When preparing the cheese for this fondue, chill it first, as it will be easiest to remove the rind if the cheese is cold. Then set it on one of its flat surfaces and slice off the rind with a sharp knife. With firmer cheeses we like to use a vegetable peeler so as to preserve more of the useable part.

$1/2$ cup plus 2 tablespoons vin santo

2 tablespoons honey

$1/4$ teaspoon anise seed

$1^1/2$ pounds Saint-André, Cowgirl Creamery Mt.Tam, or other triple-crème cheese, rind discarded and cubed

In a heavy saucepan, combine the vin santo, honey, and anise seed. Bring to a boil over high heat, then decrease the heat to low. Add the cheese to the wine mixture, a chunk at a time, whisking constantly to melt the cheese before the next addition. When all the cheese has been added, whisk until smooth. Transfer immediately to a fondue pot and serve.

Makes 3 cups

SERVE WITH: fresh or dried figs, quartered • fresh or dried pear chunks • apple chunks • toasted walnut bread cubes • fig bars • chopped toasted walnuts or hazelnuts

BEVERAGE SUGGESTIONS: vin santo • demi-sec, Champagne, or crémant (French sparkling wine) • off-dry riesling

Made for Each Other

HOMEMADE DIPPERS

Irish Brown Soda Bread

An extremely unadventurous eater as a child, Brigid remembers her visits to family in Ireland as an exercise in trying to convince her parents that she *could* live off Cadbury Fruit and Nut bars, ginger ale, and brown bread with Kerrygold butter. Although her parents didn't see eye-to-eye with her on the first two, brown bread was always plentiful, delicious, and parent approved at every meal (the butter was negotiable). Few breads require so little effort in return for such a satisfying payoff. Brown bread is actually better after it has sat for several hours, so you might want to make it a day before you plan to serve it.

2 cups unbleached all-purpose flour

2 cups whole wheat flour

1/2 cup toasted wheat germ

1/2 cup old-fashioned oats

2 tablespoons brown sugar

1 tablespoon plus 2 teaspoons kosher salt

2 teaspoons baking soda

4 ounces cold unsalted butter,
   cut into pieces

2 1/2 cups buttermilk

Preheat the oven to 400°F. Grease a baking sheet or line it with parchment paper. In a large bowl, combine the flours, wheat germ, oats, brown sugar, 1 tablespoon of the salt, and baking soda and toss to mix well. Add the butter pieces and rub into the flour mixture with your fingers until the mixture resembles coarse meal. Make a well in the center of the flour mixture and pour in the buttermilk. Stir with a wooden spoon or rubber spatula until a soft, sticky dough forms. Wet your hands slightly and gather the dough into a ball. Place it on the prepared baking sheet (if making two smaller loaves, divide the dough into two balls and place 3 to 4 inches apart on the baking sheet), shaping it into a uniform round loaf. Press on the top of the loaf to flatten it slightly. Bake until the loaf is golden brown on top and resists gentle pressure when pressed, 50 to 60 minutes. Allow the bread to cool completely on a cooling rack before cutting. Store the bread at room temperature wrapped in a kitchen towel to preserve the crust or in a freezer bag for a softer loaf. The bread will keep for several days at room temperature.

Makes one 2-pound or two 1-pound loaves

Cinnamon Sugar Doughnut Holes

Though making doughnuts may seem a little daunting, this recipe is a nice, small-scale foray into the doughnut arena, and the dough is quite forgiving.

$^3/_4$ cup warm (110°F) water

$^1/_2$ cup plus 2 tablespoons granulated sugar

1 large egg

2 tablespoons nonfat dry milk powder

1 tablespoon instant dry yeast

1 teaspoon vanilla extract

$2^1/_2$ cups all-purpose flour

2 teaspoons baking powder

6 tablespoons vegetable shortening

$1^1/_2$ teaspoons kosher salt

About 3 quarts vegetable or canola oil, for deep-frying

2 teaspoons ground cinnamon

In the bowl of a stand mixer, combine the water, 2 tablespoons of the sugar, egg, milk powder, yeast, and vanilla extract and whisk by hand until the yeast and milk powder are dissolved. Add the flour, baking powder, shortening, and salt and mix on low speed with the dough hook until the mixture comes together, about 2 minutes. Increase the speed to medium and mix until the dough is smooth and elastic, about 10 minutes. Remove the bowl from the mixer and cover it with plastic wrap. Allow the dough to sit at room temperature 20 minutes.

While the dough rests, set up the doughnut station. In a deep stockpot, pour the oil to a level of about 4 inches. Attach a candy or deep-fry thermometer to the side of the pan and set the pan over medium-low heat. Check the oil temperature frequently, lowering the heat if the oil reaches 350°F before you are ready to fry. In a small bowl, combine the remaining $^1/_2$ cup sugar with the cinnamon, mix well, and set aside. Prepare a cooling rack set atop a baking sheet or a baking sheet lined with several layers of paper towels for draining the doughnuts. You will also need a large slotted spoon or skimmer for retrieving the doughnuts from the hot oil. Line a baking sheet with parchment paper and sprinkle lightly with flour.

continued

Turn the dough out onto a floured counter or board and sprinkle with a little more flour. With a rolling pin, roll the dough to a thickness of $1/2$ inch. Pick up the edges of the dough and let it shrink back, then roll it again to $1/2$-inch thickness. With a $1^1/2$-inch-diameter round cutter, cut the dough into circles and transfer the circles to the prepared baking sheet. Press the dough scraps together and repeat the rolling and cutting process. Discard any dough left over from the second rolling.

When the oil reaches 350°F, start frying the doughnuts. Using the slotted spoon or skimmer, lower 4 or 5 dough pieces at a time into the hot oil. Don't let them touch the bottom of the pan. The dough pieces will sizzle and almost imme-diately puff up and float to the surface of the oil. As they cook, turn them over once so they brown evenly on both sides. When both sides are golden brown (the whole process takes about 1 minute), transfer the doughnuts to the cooling rack and allow them to cool slightly, then toss them in the cinnamon sugar until they are thoroughly coated. Return them to the rack to finish cooling. Repeat with the remaining doughnuts, making sure you check the oil temperature frequently, raising or lowering the heat as necessary, and waiting until the oil is the correct temperature before proceeding.

Cool the doughnuts completely and store them in a clean paper bag at room temperature until ready to serve.

Makes about 40 doughnut holes

Devil's Food Pound Cake

Chocolate cake should be, first and foremost, *chocolaty*. This cake holds up to even the sweetest fondues—try it with Yo Ho Ho and Some Coconut Rum (page 89) fondue for a Mounds Bar experience. The deep, dark, rich flavor of this chocolate cake depends on a top-quality cocoa powder, so don't skimp. We particularly recommend Scharffen Berger, Dagoba, and Bensdorp cocoa powders—look for them at well-stocked supermarkets or specialty markets.

1 1/4 cups all-purpose flour

3/4 cup cocoa powder

1/2 teaspoon kosher salt

1/4 teaspoon baking powder

1/4 teaspoon baking soda

2/3 cup water, at room temperature

1/2 teaspoon vanilla extract

5 ounces unsalted butter, at room temperature

1 cup sugar

2 large eggs

Preheat the oven to 350°F. Grease and flour an 8 by 4-inch loaf pan and set aside. In a bowl, sift together the flour, cocoa powder, salt, baking powder, and baking soda and set aside. In a small bowl, combine the water and vanilla and set aside. In a stand mixer fitted with the paddle attachment, combine the butter and sugar and beat at high speed until light and fluffy, about 2 minutes. Scrape down the mixer bowl and paddle. With the mixer running at medium speed, add the eggs, one at a time. Scrape down the bowl and paddle. Beat the egg mixture at high speed until smooth and uniform, about 1 minute. Decrease the speed to low. Add the flour mixture in three stages, alternating with the water mixture, and beginning and ending with flour. After each addition, scrape down the bowl and paddle and mix until smooth. Spread the batter in the prepared pan and bake until the top springs back when pressed lightly and a tester inserted in the cake's center comes out clean, about 55 minutes. Allow the cake to cool in the pan 10 to 20 minutes before turning it out onto a rack to cool completely.

Makes one 2-pound loaf

Sour Cream Pound Cake

Dense, rich, and sturdy, pound cake is the perfect dessert fondue dipper. With its delicious sour cream tang, this cake also pairs well with fresh fruit and ice cream.

1³/₄ cups sifted cake flour

¹/₄ teaspoon baking soda

¹/₄ teaspoon kosher salt

4 ounces unsalted butter, at room temperature

1¹/₂ cups granulated sugar

3 large eggs, at room temperature

2 teaspoons vanilla extract

¹/₂ cup sour cream, at room temperature

Preheat oven to 350°F. Grease and flour an 8 by 4-inch loaf pan. In a bowl, sift together the flour, baking soda, and salt and set aside. In a stand mixer fitted with the paddle attachment, beat the butter and sugar at high speed until very light and fluffy, 3 to 4 minutes. Scrape down the mixer bowl and paddle. In a bowl, combine the eggs and vanilla. With the mixer at medium speed, add the egg mixture gradually, increasing the speed if the batter looks curdled. When all the egg mixture has been added, scrape down the bowl and paddle. With the mixer at high speed, mix 30 seconds more. Decrease the speed to low. Add the flour mixture in three stages, alternating with the sour cream, and beginning and ending with flour. After each addition, scrape down the bowl and paddle and mix until smooth. Spread the batter in the prepared pan and bake until the top springs back when pressed lightly and a tester inserted in the cake's center comes out clean, about 50 minutes. Allow the cake to cool in the pan for 10 to 20 minutes before turning out onto a rack to cool completely.

Makes one 2-pound loaf

Mango Marshmallows

We call for mangoes here, but experiment with different fruits for your various fondue adventures. Substitute raspberries or blackberries for a great accompaniment to dark chocolate fondues, or strawberries for milk chocolate. For plain marshmallows, replace the fruit puree with 3/4 cup water and 2 teaspoons vanilla extract. The marshmallows must sit out at room temperature for 10 to 12 hours, so it's best to make them at least a day before you plan to serve them.

6 ounces (1 cup) frozen mangoes, strawberries, or a combination, thawed

1 tablespoon fresh lime juice

1/2 cup plus 2 tablespoons water

2 (1/4-ounce) packets unflavored gelatin

1 1/2 cups granulated sugar

1/2 cup plus 2 tablespoons light corn syrup

1/4 teaspoon kosher salt

Confectioners' sugar, for coating marshmallows

In a blender or food processor, puree the thawed fruit with the lime juice until completely smooth. Strain the puree through a fine mesh strainer. You should end up with 1/2 cup of thick puree. In the bowl of a stand mixer, combine the puree and 1/4 cup of the water, then sprinkle the gelatin on top. Fit the mixer with the whip attachment.

Line a 13 by 9-inch baking pan with aluminum foil and coat the foil with vegetable oil or nonstick spray. Attach a candy thermometer to the side of a heavy saucepan. Combine the remaining 1/4 cup plus 2 tablespoons of water, the sugar, corn syrup, and salt in the saucepan and bring to a boil over high heat. Cook the sugar mixture to 240°F and remove from the heat. With the mixer running at medium-high speed, pour the hot syrup in a thin stream slowly down the side of the mixer bowl, avoiding the whip. When all the syrup has been added, increase the mixer speed to high and whip until the mixture is very fluffy and stiff, about 8 minutes. Pour the mixture into the prepared pan and smooth with

continued

an oiled offset spatula. Allow the mixture to sit, uncovered, at room temperature for 10 to 12 hours.

Sift confectioners' sugar generously over the marshmallow slab. Turn it out onto a cutting board or counter, peel off the foil, and dust it with more sugar. Slice the marshmallows with an oiled thin-bladed knife or oiled cookie cutters. Dip all the cut edges in confectioners' sugar, shaking off any excess. The marshmallows will keep several weeks at room temperature in an airtight container.

Makes about forty-eight 1$^1/_2$ inch-square marshmallows

RESOURCES

E-commerce has done wonders for those of us who live in places where the most exotic cheese in the market comes in a green can. Here are a few website and catalog sources (some have brick-and-mortar options) that will satisfactorily meet most of your fondue needs.

CHEESES AND OTHER FOODS

Capri Flavors
Retail store/online catalog
www.capriflavors.com
800-861-5440
Italian cheeses, dried and preserved fruits (amarena cherries), biscotti, and everything else Italian

The Cheese Cellar
Retail store/online catalog
www.thecheesecellar.com
206-404-2743
Cheeses

CheeseSupply.com
Online catalog
www.cheesesupply.com
866-205-6376
Cheeses and cheesemaking supplies

Chocosphere
Online catalog
www.chocosphere.com
877-992-4626
Amazing chocolate selection

Cowgirl Creamery
Retail stores/online catalog
www.cowgirlcreamery.com
866-433-7834
Cheeses (including Pantaleo),
condiments, and accessories for serving
cheese

Dorothy Lane Market
Retail stores/online catalog
www.dlmmailorder.com
866-748-1391
Artisan bread, cheeses, and specialty
items

Formaggio Kitchen
Retail stores/online catalog
www.formaggio-kitchen.com
888-212-3224
Cheeses (including Pantaleo),
specialty items

Futters Nut Butters
Online catalog
www.futtersnutbutters.com
877-772-2155
Hazelnut butter

Gourmet Food Store
Online catalog
www.gourmetfoodstore.com
877-591-8008
Cheeses, specialty meats, and treats

igourmet.com
Online catalog
www.igourmet.com
877-446-8763
Cheeses, chocolate, marcona almonds,
harissa, and other international specialty
items

Murray's Cheese
Retail stores/online and direct-mail
catalogs
www.murrayscheese.com
888-692-4339
Probably the best selection of cheeses
by mail in the country

ShopNatural
Online catalog
www.shopnatural.com
520-884-0745
Hazelnut butter, chocolate, natural and
organic products

The Spanish Table
Retail stores/online catalog
www.spanishtable.com
206-682-2827
Food (including pimentón and marcona almonds), wine, cookware, and more from Spain and Portugal

Zabar's
Retail store/online and direct-mail catalogs
www.zabars.com
800-697-6301
Cheeses, chocolate, specialty items, artisan breads

Zingerman's
Retail store/online and direct-mail catalogs
www.zingermans.com
888-636-8162
Cheeses, pimentón, chocolate, artisan breads, and a well-chosen variety of other delicious products

FONDUE POTS AND ACCESSORIES

Amazon.com
www.amazon.com
What *don't* they have? Fondue pots, fuel, cheeses (sold through some of the merchants listed here), harissa, and chocolate

Chef's Resource
Online catalog
www.chefsresource.com
866-765-2499
Fondue pots and fuel

Cooking.com
Online catalog
www.cooking.com
800-663-8810
Huge selection of fondue pots and fuel

Dean and DeLuca
Retail stores/online and direct-mail catalogs
www.deandeluca.com
800-221-7714
Cheeses, chocolate, fondue pots and accessories

eBay
www.ebay.com
Lenny swears by it for all her fabulous vintage fondue sets

Marshalls, Ross, TJ Maxx, and Tuesday Morning
Retail stores/online catalogs
www.marshallsonline.com
800-627-7425
www.rossstores.com
800-945-7677
www.tjmaxx.com
800-285-6299
www.tuesdaymorning.com
972-387-3562, ext.7888
Bargain fondue pots and fun party accessories

Sur La Table
Retail stores/online and direct-mail catalogs
www.surlatable.com
800-843-0852
Fondue pots and accessories

Williams-Sonoma
Retail stores/online and direct-mail catalogs
www.williamssonoma.com
877-812-6235
Fondue pots, accessories, and cheeses

WINES

If you live in one of the states to which wine can be shipped directly by mail, you've got a whole other world of wine options at your fingertips. These are a few of the many wine buying websites recommended to us by our friend Peter Marks, who is a Master of Wine and the Senior Director of Wine and Food at COPIA: The American Center for Wine, Food, and the Arts, not to mention the world's greatest teller of awful jokes. Even though he drinks—we mean TASTES—a lot we still trust his judgment!

Bounty Hunter Rare Wines
& Provisions
www.bountyhunterwine.com
800-943-9463

Brown Derby International
Wine Center
www.brownderby.com
800-491-3438

K and L Wine Merchants
www.klwines.com
877-559-4637

North Coast Wine Group
www.winebyphone.com
877-946-3590

Sam's Wines and Spirits
www.samswine.com
800-777-9137

SelectWinesLLC.com
www.selectwinesllc.com
888-421-9463

wine.com
www.wine.com
800-592-5870

wineanthology.com
www.wineanthology.com
888-238-2251

The Wine Buyer
www.thewinebuyer.com
973-872-0275

Zachys
www.zachys.com
866-922-4971

Index